Acknowledgements	i
Foreword	iii
Preface	iv
Introduction	xi
Family and Early Life	1
Answering the Call	21
Path to the Pulpit	31
The Facts of Life	51
Paths and Pitfalls	59
A Time of Change	71
Far from Home	81
Photographs	95
Finding My Place	111
Married, with Children — and a Church	129
Raising a Family, Leading a Flock	145
Growing in Faith	161
"As For Me and My House…"	171
Appendices	177
The Truth about Black History in the Bible	178
On the Importance of Bible Training and Education	181
On Marriage	185
The Serviceman's Family	189
Address to the 1960 National Baptist Convention	195
On Missionary Work	199
More Reflections on Pain and Loss: The Story of Ruth	211
The Black Church	215
Our Roots	219

Life's Crossroad to Destiny

Reverend Dr. Samuel Berthal Joubert, Sr.

Welstar Publications ✳ Brooklyn, NY

Copyright © 2008 by Welstar Publications.

All rights reserved. No part of this publication may be reproduced, stored in a retrieval system, or transmitted in any form or by any means electronic, mechanical, photocopying, recording or otherwise, without the written permission of Welstar Publications.

All Biblical quotations are taken from the King James Version (KJV) unless otherwise identified.

Written by Reverend Dr. Samuel Berthal Joubert Sr., with K. J. McElrath.

Published by Welstar Publications, Inc.
628 Lexington Avenue, Brooklyn, NY 11221.
Phone: (718) 453-6557, Fax: (718) 338-1454.
E-mail to drbatson@optonline.com
or editor@welstarpublications.com

ISBN: 0-938503-37-5
10 9 8 7 6 5 4 3 2 1

Cover Design by G. Lynas, NYC
Text set in Book Antiqua

Editing/Book Design
By Karen Babcock and Robert Hayes

Typography
By Karen Babcock

ACKNOWLEDGEMENTS

This book is dedicated to my dearly beloved, Bible-believing Christian mother, Mrs. Virgie E. Wickliffe Joubert, who nurtured me in the word of God from childhood up, along with my grandmothers, Elmira Robert Wickliffe and Florestine Adoine Joubert. It is also dedicated to my oldest sister, Clara Joubert Alexander, who was like a second mother to me, and last but by no means least, to my darling Life Companion of sixty years of marriage, Rev. Doris Thorpe Joubert Sr.

Above all I owe an unending debt of gratitude, love and appreciation to God my Heavenly Father for my five offspring and their families: Rev. Samuel Joubert Jr., wife Susan Joubert, and daughter Cassandra; Mr. David Eugene Joubert Sr., wife Phyllis McKoy Joubert, and their son David Eugene Joubert Jr., daughter-in-law Audrey Joubert, and daughter Angele Estella Joubert; my daughter Deborah Elizabeth Joubert McCampbell and her husband, Rev. Charles McCampbell Sr., and their sons Charles, Kevin, Caleb, and Christopher McCampbell and daughter Charla and her husband Sergio Moreno; Charles Jr. and his wife Carrie; my son Joseph Edward Joubert, wife Renay Peters Joubert; and my son Rev. Dr. Phillip Charles Joubert Sr. and his wife, Rev. Gala Derene Joubert, and their children Phillip Charles Joubert Jr., Joseph Edward Joubert II, Matthew Brown Bolden

Joubert, Bethany Gala Derene Joubert, Mark Jefferson Berthal Joubert, and Berea Doris Allean Joubert.

This book is written as a result of my early boyhood experience as well as a strong desire early in life to write a book. The title was originally to be *Life's Crossroad to Success*. However, it finally occurred to me that such a book would take years of experience to write. In addition, success is a term that is relative to each individual. Consequently the title has been changed to *Life's Crossroad to Destiny*.

This book is truly the index of my life's experience and my basic fundamental belief and practice — keeping Christ central in my life.

FOREWORD

By Rev. Dr. H. Devore Chapman

We thank God for Rev. Dr. Samuel B. Joubert, Sr.!

This book gives us an opportunity to be close to the experience, exposure, and the excitement of this rich and rewarding ministry. We see the good news of the Gospel from cover to cover. This work shows us the value of faith, family, fellowship, and faithfulness. We praise God for the wisdom, the wit, and the work. This is a great expression of a marvelous life. This is a must for preachers, pastors, and Christian leaders. This is a refreshing, revealing, and passionate work of a gospel preacher. I personally thank him for friendship, fellowship, and a ministerial model for pastors, preachers, and Christ-loving people. Dr. Samuel Joubert Sr. – man of God, father, husband, grandfather, prophet, seer, watchman, worker, believer. Read and be blessed!

Rev. Dr. H. Devore Chapman is Pastor of the Greater Bright Light Missionary Baptist Church and the Bethel Baptist Church, Recording Secretary of the National Baptist Convention U.S.A. Inc., former Moderator of the Eastern Baptist Association and one of Dr. Joubert's sons in the Spirit.

Preface
My Basic, Fundamental Belief

That readers may have a clear picture and understanding of me, from whence I come in all I have said and done in this life, I hereby set forth my personal statement of faith:

I believe the teachings of the Holy Bible.

I believe that there is one and only one Living and True God, an Infinite, Intelligent Spirit whose Name is Jehovah, Maker and Supreme Ruler of Heaven and Earth, inexpressibly glorious in His Holiness, worthy of all possible honor, confidence, and love.

I believe that in the Unity of the Godhead, there are three Divine Persons: the Father, the Son, and the Holy Spirit; I believe they are equal in every divine aspect of perfection their respective execution of distinct, yet harmonious offices in the great Work of Redemption for Mankind.

Theological Definitions of God

1. "God is a Spirit, Infinite, Eternal and unchanging in His being, wisdom, holiness, justice, goodness and truth."
   —the *Westminster Shorter Catechism*

2. "God is an Eternal Personal Being of absolute knowledge, power and goodness."
—John Miley,
American Theologian (1813–1895)

3. "God is the Infinite and Perfect Spirit in whom all things have their source, support and end."
—Augustus H. Strong,
American Theologian (1836–1921)

On Creation

Creation may be defined as what the great nineteenth- and early twentieth-century Baptist theologian Augustus Hopkins Strong described as "that free act of the Triune God by which in the beginning and for His own glory he made, with out the use of pre-existing material, the whole visible and invisible Universe."

God is the Author of Creation, acting through the twofold agency of the Word and the Spirit. More specifically, each aspect of the work of Creation is ascribed to each of the Three Divine Personages of the Trinity. Thus, in Creation:

- The Father conceives (Genesis 1:1, 1 Corinthians 8:6, and Colossians 1:16)
- The Son executes (John 1:3, 1 Corinthians 8:6, Colossians 1:16, and Hebrews 1:2 and 11:3)
- The Holy Spirit completes (Genesis 1:2 and Job 26:13 and 33:4)

I stand firm on the teaching of the Bible, which states that Man was created in the image of God. According to Genesis 1:26–27:

> *Then God said, Let us make Man in our Image, in our Likeness, and let him rule over the fish of the sea and the birds of the air, over the livestock, over all the earth, and over all the creatures that move along the ground.*
>
> *So God created Man in His own Image; in the Image of God He created them; male and female he created them.*

The terms "image" and "likeness" are synonymous in both the Old and the New Testament. The concept includes such characteristics as righteousness and holiness (Ephesians 4:24) and knowledge (Colossians 3:10).

All very well and good… but what exactly does being made in the image of God really mean?

God is a Trinity, meaning Three Parts making up One Triune God. It means that God made Man likewise in Trinity forms: three parts that make up a whole Man or Being. The Scripture that speaks of the trinity of Man is found in I Thessalonians 5:23, which says: "May the very God of Peace sanctify you wholly: and I pray God your whole spirit and soul and body be preserved blameless unto the coming of our Lord, Jesus Christ."

As Above, So Within

Man is made with a body. In the 139th Psalm, David the Shepherd King praises the Lord:

> *For you created my inmost being; you knit me together in my mother's womb. I praise You because I am fearfully and wonderfully made; Your Works are Wonderful, I know that full well.*
>
> *My frame was not hidden from you when I was made in the secret place. When I was woven together in the depths of the earth, Your eyes saw my unformed body.*
>
> *All the days ordained for me were written in Your book before one of them came to be.*

Man is made with a spirit. In Hebrews 4:12, we read:

> *For the Word of God is living and active. Sharper than any double-edged sword, it penetrates even to dividing soul and spirit, joints and marrow; it judges the thoughts and attitudes of the heart.*

The Spirit of Man is the center of our intellect, that which controls our wills and actions. In the Bible, the words "spirit" and "heart" are often used in the same context. It is in the spirit, or heart, of Man that sin finds its starting place. In the Gospel of Mark, 7:21–26, Jesus says: "All these evils come from inside and make a man unclean."

It is also in the heart of a Man that Salvation begins. Consider Romans 6:17:

> *Thanks be to God that though you be slaves to sin, you wholeheartedly obeyed the form of teaching*

to which you were entrusted. You have been set free from sin and have become slaves to righteousness.

The natural man's spirit is hard to control, because he doesn't have the indwelling help of the Holy Spirit. He is not right-thinking, because his heart, or spirit, isn't right with God.

Man is made with a soul. According to Genesis 2:7, God breathed into Man the breath of life, and Man became a living soul:

> *The Lord God formed the Man from the dust of the ground and breathed into his nostrils the breath of life, and the Man became a living soul.*

The soul is the seat of all affections, emotions, and desires. It is the soul of man that co-ordinates the thoughts of the spirit (heart) of man and the activities of the body of man.

Now, when we read the Scripture that says Man is made in the image of God, we are made to understand that Man is body, soul, and spirit. The Spirit tells the Soul what to do, the Soul then tells the Body what to do, and the Body takes action in response.

The Price of Sin

In Man's original state, having been made in the image and likeness of God, he was righteous, innocent, without sin, and in perfect communion with God. Then, in Genesis 2:16–17:

> *The Lord God commanded the man, You are free to eat from any tree in the garden, but you must not eat from the Tree of the Knowledge of Good and Evil.*
>
> *For when you eat of it, you shall surely die.*

The man Adam to whom God gave this command is the federal head of the human race, or human family. Adam failed the test and disobeyed God by eating of the fruit of the tree from which he was explicitly told not to eat. Consequently, Adam sinned against God his Creator and became alienated from God. He was no longer righteous, holy, innocent, and in perfect communion with God.

The umbilical cord was cut when Adam sinned. Since Adam is the federal head of the human family—meaning that the seed of Adam is within each and every one of us at birth—we are all born sinners and need to be reconciled to God our Maker.

The penalty for sin is Death and eternal Hell.

Who Pays the Price

Now, to make a long story short and to the point, the only One who met the qualification required by God the Father—and who could therefore make things right on our behalf, making it possible for Man to be brought back in reconciliation with the Father—was Jesus Christ, God's only begotten Son.

Jesus was at once very much God and very much Man.

Consider that Adam was made a living soul

(Genesis 2:7). Jesus was made a "quickening," or life-giving, spirit. The contrast here between the natural body and the spiritual body follows from their two representatives.

In the Beginning, Adam had a natural body of the dust of the ground (Genesis 2:7). At the end, Jesus had the body of life-giving spirit (John 5:26 and 6:26). Through His death and resurrection at the Second Coming, He will give to his redeemed People a spiritual body: physical, yet imperishable, without corruption and adaptable for life in the presence of God forever (Philippians 3:21).

It will be a body similar to that of Christ: resurrected, glorified and physical.

The Eternal Reward

Adam, the earthly man, and all his descendants received natural, earthly bodies. Christ, the Man from Heaven who became incarnate in a human body, received a glorified spiritual body upon his resurrection; so too will all His Redeemed people receive a spiritual body at the End of Days.

Amen.

Rev. Dr. Samuel B. Joubert, Sr.

INTRODUCTION

Like many children, I suffered from tonsillitis throughout my tender years. However, our doctor told my parents not to have them removed until I was older.

By that time I was nine years old—this was in 1931—and my tonsils were getting so badly inflamed that our family doctor decided it was time to take them out. Since my mother was also in need of a medical procedure, it was decided that we should ride the train (the way most people traveled in those days) some two hundred miles from our home in Grand Prairie in order to receive treatment at the Charity Hospital in New Orleans.

My tonsillectomy was scheduled for the day after we arrived, and I confess I was a most uncooperative patient. Ultimately, the surgeon and his assistants had to strap me down to the table in order to do their work.

Being young and healthy, I recovered quickly, but as my mother's surgery had not yet been scheduled (and those being the days when hospitals in America were actually there to help those in need), I was allowed to stay until my mother was ready to return home.

There was a small play area in front of the hospital with benches and a fountain with small fish swimming around. One day during this period I was out there playing with a white boy about my age. He was friendly enough; we were standing there by the fountain, watching the fish when suddenly he reached down and splashed water into my face.

I might have been puny and small for my age, but I was as strong as an ox—all through my life I'd whipped all the boys my age and even some a little older, and I sure wasn't going to take it from this one.

By the time I'd wiped the water out of my eyes, the white boy had disappeared. I was too young in those days to understand the consequences of a black boy beating up a white boy in that culture—I just knew I was going to pay him back.

Since I couldn't see him, I started to walk away, then stumbled over him—he'd been lying flat on the ground, hiding. I lunged for him, determined to teach him a lesson, when suddenly two strong hands closed around my arms. I felt myself being picked up, and in the next moment, I was looking into the face of a tall, fatherly-looking black man who'd been seated on a nearby bench watching me.

"Boy, do you want to start a race riot? You leave that white boy alone!"

That kindly gentleman proceeded to give me a short course on the reality of black/white race relations. It opened my eyes to the hard truth of how us "coloreds" were viewed by white people.

Only the good Lord knows what might have happened to me had that gentleman not been sitting there. Some folks think of angels as these glorious beings with wings and brilliant white robes with halos around their heads, but I'm here to tell you that angels are always walking among us in disguise, watching over us—just like that gentleman who stopped me from doing something that day that would have had very bad consequences not only for me, but the entire black community.

Today, I still thank the Lord for that early lesson—that not everyone who grins in your face is necessarily your friend, and that someone who holds one hand out in friendship may be hiding a bludgeon or a knife behind his back with the other.

I learned something else that day: God, the Sovereign Head Creator and Sustainer of the Universe, loves us all—even a poor, colored boy from the backwoods of St. Landry Parish, Louisiana.

This is the unfolding of my life story and my Christian journey—a journey that has made me who I am and, despite the hateful ways of the world, will not allow me to hate or mistreat any man, be he white, black or yellow, Jewish, Christian or Muslim, Irish, Italian, or Chinese—for all are Children of God, and what we do to another we do to Him.

Chapter I
Family and Early Life

When people think about the 1920s, most of them think about jazz, parties, bathtub gin, and dances like the "Charleston" (which black people had been dancing for twenty years before white people had even heard of it). Some of the greatest African-American artistic achievements were accomplished during that period that some people call "The Jazz Age"—up in Harlem, African-Americans like writer Langston Hughes, artist Augusta Savage and composer Duke Ellington were creating a vibrant community and culture that was uniquely African-American.

This was not the reality for most blacks in the USA at the time—and particularly not for poor blacks in the South.

My Heritage

We were luckier than most—the land on which we lived and worked belonged to my paternal grandmother, Florestine Joubert. Grandmother Florestine was what folks in Louisiana called "quadroon," meaning one of her grandparents was black, making her one-quarter African by descent. She was a stunning woman with deep blue eyes and rich, long, black hair. As a widow, she inherited 365 acres with five houses on it when my grandfather, Edmond

Joubert Jr., was murdered by a highway robber.

My maternal grandmother, Elmira Wickliffe, was what folks in those days called *mulatto*—product of a white father and a black mother. She had dark blonde hair, gray eyes, and a wicked sense of humor.

I go into this because it's important to understand that unlike most of the South, "race" in old Louisiana was a very complex issue that went far beyond simple "black and white." Had my grandmother Florestine not had as much white blood as she did, it's unlikely she would have owned any land at all. It's also worth noting that while the early French settlers could be just as racist in their way as other whites, this racism took a different form. Instead of passing laws and persecuting and excluding people with dark skin, French people decided the solution was to intermarry with them and turn them into Frenchmen.

The bottom line was we had a place to be on land owned by the family in a house that was bigger and nicer than that in which most poor blacks in the rural South had to live. We turned a quarter of all the produce we grew and all the money we earned over to Grandmother Florestine—the rest belonged to us, which was a far better situation than that faced by most Southern black sharecroppers.

It also meant access to a better education. My mother, Virgie, was a schoolteacher. Although pay for schoolteachers was poor in those days (how little things have changed!), her income helped supplement what we received from the farm, which was managed by my father, Edmond Joubert III.

What was significant about my mother's side of the

family is that it was a family of preachers. Her father—my grandfather—was the Reverend Samuel Wickliffe, who died at a relatively young age. Two of his sons—my uncles Samuel (Jr.) and Hayward—followed in Grandfather Wickliffe's footsteps into the service of the Lord.

This is the background of the family into which I was born Samuel Berthal Joubert on April 28, 1922, the fifth of eight children who survived infancy.

My Birth

It was a quiet spring afternoon—about 4 in the afternoon, to the best of my parents' recollection—when I arrived. The doctor who delivered me was a white man named Dr. Batt. He had arrived by horse and buggy, as doctors had for a hundred years or more. Even though automobiles had been around for a while, few people in our part of the country—rich, poor, black or white—owned one, because even if you could afford one, there were very few paved roads outside of the city.

It was also customary in those days to have present at the birthing a midwife, who was generally an elderly black woman.

My papa was proud as he held me in his arms. "What do you think?" he asked the midwife.

The midwife shook her head and said, "He's a mite ugly."

From that point forward, my father had very little to say to that woman.

My Extended Family

I mentioned that I had eight brothers and sisters, but it is important to understand that in those days, the definition of "family" was much broader. Today, it's popular to talk about the "traditional family" as the mother, father and children—in other words, the "nuclear" family. Back in those days, however, most people outside of cities had extended families that included not only mothers, fathers, brothers, and sisters, but also grandparents, aunts, uncles, and cousins.

The Joubert family even now is more of an extended family than a nuclear one, but this was especially true back in those days. Although we didn't all live under one roof, most of us lived on the same land, and we were all very close. Two of my cousins were especially close to me—we were more like brothers than cousins—and they would play a significant role throughout my life.

More on My Forebears

I have previously mentioned my paternal grandmother, Florestine, who came into ownership of the family property when my grandfather, Edmond Joubert Jr., was killed by a highway robber.

The way the story was told to me, it happened the day that he took his last bale of cotton to the cotton gin, where he received payment for all the bales produced that year. Every year, he would drive into the town of Washington ten miles away and pay off his debt to the commissary store there—carrying his entire year's income on his person.

My father was to have gone with him that day. Had he done so, I might not be here today to tell the story.

A man in our area had been keeping tabs on my grandfather, noting the time of his comings and goings. He hid behind a tree that day, waiting for my grandfather to pass by on his way from the cotton gin into town. When my grandfather drove by, the robber shot him dead with a shotgun.

The force of the shells knocked my grandfather off the seat and onto the ground; the noise frightened the horses so badly that they took off for home with my grandfather's wagon behind them.

When he searched my grandfather's pockets, his killer found thirteen cents. Wisely, my grandfather had hidden all the bills in a packet underneath the commodities he was carrying in the back of the wagon.

My father's brothers—my uncles—were Leon, Christoval, and Alcide; his sisters were young Florestine, Celestine, Edmonia, Angel, and Christelia. Uncle Leon, also a deacon, was one of the first in our family to own an automobile, a Model T Ford.

He was killed driving it one day after returning from visiting his daughter and son-in-law; the road crossed a branch line of the Louisiana & Arkansas Railway, which ran from New Orleans, through Baton Rouge, and through our area up to Alexandria and points beyond. As he was approaching the crossing that day, a train was coming. Braking a Model T Ford was a tricky proposition; there were three pedals that had to be applied in a certain way.

My Uncle Leon saw the train bearing down on the crossing and apparently panicked, stepping on the wrong pedals and causing the car to leap forward—right into the path of the oncoming train.

God be praised, he didn't suffer much.

My maternal grandfather was also a pastor. Originally from Kentucky, Reverend Samuel Wickliffe Sr. also died prematurely, being carried off by pneumonia at the relatively young age of fifty. My mother's brothers were Alonzo, Samuel Jr., and Hayward (who as mentioned earlier also became preachers), and Robert; Mama's sisters were Aurelia, Estella, Elsa, Virginia, and Clara.

My grandmother Elmira was born in the town of Cheneyville, about halfway between Grand Prairie and Alexandria. By the time she had married and started a family with Samuel Wickliffe, the family was living in the town of Evergreen, about ten miles away.

My Immediate Family

As you recall, my mother was a schoolteacher. She had the privilege of receiving a fine education, graduating from the Gilbert Academy of New Orleans, a secondary school run under the auspices of New Orleans University.

The Lord works in strange and wondrous ways; it was her education and her profession that brought her into my father's life. In Grand Prairie, when my father was born in the late nineteenth century, there were no schools for "colored" people. Understanding that education was the only way to advance our people, my great-uncle, Louis Joubert (Grandfather Edmond's brother) initiated the idea of finding a teacher and opening a school for black children.

After an extensive search, he found my mother and convinced her to become the school's first teacher. My father was a young man by then. He led the project to cut and mill the lumber from which the new schoolhouse would be built. Meanwhile, Virgie was given lodgings in my great-uncle's home.

My father was a strong and hardworking man, but had not had the opportunity to get an education as a boy. However, the feeling was that it was never too late to start; my father was one of Mama's first students. He was a handsome young man, and Mama was an attractive young woman with a full, fine figure; nature being what it is, it didn't take long for Papa to become "teacher's pet."

There was only one problem, at first: Mama had already been "going steady" with a young man from her hometown of Evergreen. However, when Grandmother Elmira met my father, she immediately claimed him as her son-in-law to be.

And you *know* the rest of the story.

When Mama smiled, it was like a ray of sunshine. She was a strong woman, not afraid of anyone; she "covered every inch of the ground on which she stood."

She was a cook *par excellence* and could sing, teach, and pray with the finest preachers I have ever known. She devoted much of her spare time visiting and praying for the sick; many were healed as the Lord worked through her.

As well as being as strong as an ox and as hardworking as a mule, Papa was a devout man who attended church every Sunday without fail. He taught me how to work and of the importance of being independent by earning my own keep. Laziness was to Papa an abomination.

The first child born to my parents was named "Boy Blue." He died either in childbirth, or shortly thereafter; it was all too common to lose a child in those days before modern medical services were widely available. My eldest brother was Eldridge Kermit. Next came my two older sisters: Clara Eulalee and Angel Estella. As was common in large families of those days, Clara was to assume a great deal of responsibility in my upbringing; she was in many ways a second mother to me.

The children who came after me were my little brother, Edmo Ethelbert, my sister Ruthie and the baby of the family, Rupert. Edmo and Ruthie were very special to me, but sadly, they would not survive childhood; for whatever His reasons, the Lord decided he wanted Edmo and Ruthie by His side, sparing them the trials and tribulations of earthly life.

Our Home

The place where we lived was called Grand Prairie, located about ten miles northwest of the town of Washington, Louisiana, in the parish of St. Landry. Although you'll still find it on maps, it has never been an incorporated town; today, as then, it is made up primarily of family farms, although the thick woodlands I grew up among have largely disappeared.

The country house in which I was born and raised had a living room, a kitchen, two bedrooms, and an upstairs loft. As was the case for all homes in the country in those days, we had an outdoor privy; for bathing, we heated water on the wood-fired stove and poured it into a big metal or wooden wash tub.

There was also an upstairs attic, or loft; this was used for the storage of cotton seed (our primary cash crop) as well as various commodities such as cans of syrup and lard, cornmeal, flour, peanuts, various canned goods, smoked ham, and salt pork—basically, any foods that could be preserved and stored for the long term. Before President Franklin Roosevelt passed the Rural Electrification Act of 1936, virtually *nobody* who lived outside big cities had electricity—and since we lived five miles from the nearest town and there were no paved roads and no motor trucks to carry ice, having an icebox was not an option as it might have been in the city.

Despite the fact that Mama had her hands full with eight children, she kept an impeccably clean house and made certain we children were all well fed.

Outside, our country home had a picket fence that surrounded the entire house. Three small gates—one in the front, one in back, and one on the side—allowed entrance and egress; the side gate opened into the barnyard, which was surrounded by a wire fence. This is where the well stood, from which we drew our water with a bucket tied to a rope.

In front of the house was a beautiful, fragrant jasmine shrub on which white flowers would bloom every spring, giving off the most enchanting scent. On one side of the house next to the picket fence was a mulberry tree. There were also several peach trees around the yard, as well as a pecan tree.

My sister Clara was the family landscape designer. She kept the yard looking beautiful with various kinds of flowers, which included sunflowers, four o'clock flowers, and several rosebushes. Honeysuckle grew up and around the posts that supported the roof over the porch.

The barn provided shelter for our animals as well as storage for our produce: corn, hay, soybeans and feed for our livestock. In those days, the term "horsepower" was quite literal; the horses that powered our plow and the buggy in which we traveled lived in two stalls, while the buggy itself was stored in a shed adjoining the barn.

The family privy, or outhouse, was located at the far end of the barnyard, as far from the house as possible. In the days before indoor plumbing, this was the only option for rural families, even if you were rich. Our outhouse was probably as nice as such a building could be, with a goodly amount of room; it was ten feet tall, three feet wide and sat above a good, *deep* hole. I don't need to go into the description much; we've all made use of one at some point.

The barnyard had its own gates, one of which opened into the fields where we grew our produce. The other led to a pasture where our horses and mules grazed. Sometimes the cows joined them; more often, they grazed in the woods or by the roadside.

Family and Early Life

Growing Up

As I said earlier, we were luckier than most rural black families in the South. We may not have been rich (although with my Grandmother Florestine's land holdings, she could be considered reasonably wealthy), but we didn't go hungry. On our farm there were horses, mules, cows, chickens, geese, and pigs as well as dogs and cats (which were *not* allowed in the house, but could share the porch on occasion). In addition to the land on which we grew our cash crops—okra, black-eyed peas, sweet potatoes, white potatoes, cotton, corn, sugar cane, pumpkins, and melons—as well as walnut, pecan, and numerous fruit trees, we had a kitchen garden where we grew lettuce, mustard and beet greens, string and butter beans, and sugar peas.

The woods and the bayous around our home were equally bounteous. Today, one is obliged to pay for a license to hunt and fish, and only during certain times of the year. The forests that were once available for all to use are now owned by people who fence those trees and lock them with a gate, and those without a key who presume to enter are liable to be arrested as trespassers.

It was not that way when I was a youth; anyone could go fishing or hunting for venison, or gather moss from the trees that could be sold for thirty or forty cents a pound for mattress stuffing and other domestic uses.

Although I remember childhood as generally being pleasant, there was tragedy as well. As a young boy, I was blessed with a younger brother named Edmo and a little sister named Ruthie. Edmo took after our Grandmother Elmira, sharing her light complexion and blue-gray eyes; Ruthie was as much a beauty as our Grandmother Florestine, with the same long black hair. Being too young for school, they would watch me when I left for the schoolhouse in the morning and would run out to meet me in the pasture when I returned in the evening.

The Lord took them both from us one winter when I was about seven. A pneumonia epidemic swept through our community. I can never forget that dark, cloudy day when their bodies were placed in small wooden caskets and taken to the church for the funeral and burial. I was not allowed to go; I stood on the porch and watched the wagon carrying their bodies as it traveled up the road and out of sight.

At that age, I did not understand the reality of death. Every day after that, I would stand out on the porch, expecting Edmo and Ruthie to return the same way they had left—until Mama realized what I was doing. She took me on her lap and, calling me by her pet name for me said, "Bertie… they're not coming back. They've gone to be with the Lord up there in heaven where we'll all go to meet them some day."

There were times when I think *I* am lucky to have survived childhood. Of course, I now know that "luck" had less to do with it than the fact that the Lord God was keeping an eye out for me.

One Sunday morning—I was about seven or eight years old at the time—my brother Eldridge, who was fourteen, decided to get in some exercise before church by cutting a tree in the nearby woods. He took out Papa's good wood chopping ax, hefted it onto his broad shoulders, and strode on into the forest.

Unknown to Eldridge, I was following him from a distance in order to see what he was up to.

My brother selected a medium-sized tree and started to hack away. I sneaked into the thicket, standing behind him so I could get a better look at what he was doing. Out of curiosity, I moved closer... closer...

Finally, I poked my head out in order to watch the wood chips falling—just at the time Eldridge was drawing back for another swing.

WHAM! The blunt end of that ax whacked me right in the head—just above my right eye. The top of the axe-handle punctured the flesh under the eyebrow, and blood came pouring out like water out of a pump.

By the time we reached the house, my eye had completely swollen shut and looked like a black, blue, and red balloon. Seeing us, Mama screamed in horror: *"Look what you done to my Bertie!"*

My parents loaded me into our buggy, and Papa got those horses running for all they were worth as they rushed me to the nearest doctor. The doctor administered first aid and bandaged it in order to prevent an infection from setting in.

My eye remained swollen and shut for many days afterward. Mama was worried that my eye had been crushed, that I would be half-blind and left with a disfiguring scar for the rest of my life. One night, however, the Lord sent me a vision in a dream—the first of many He would grant me throughout my life.

In the dream, I saw myself healed and whole, with two good eyes and no trace of a scar.

There was another incident when I was about thirteen. My brother Eldridge—by that time he was a full-grown man at age twenty—and I had spent the morning plowing the field and were heading indoors for our noontime dinner. Eldridge was in front, leading our mule Henry, and I was following, riding on back of the horse Daisy. Both animals were wearing their harness collars—the kind with two prongs sticking up about five inches or so where the neck meets the shoulder—and bridles with all the reins in place.

Being a mischievous boy, I threw Daisy's reins over at Henry. Daisy's reins got hung up on the prongs of Henry's harness collar; this spooked the mule, and he jumped forward.

Unfortunately, Daisy didn't move. But the force of Henry leaping forward threw the poor mare off balance, and down she fell onto the wire fence—with me still on her back!

Daisy went down, landing hard on my left leg, which became tangled in the wire fence. It all happened in the space of two or three seconds—no more.

Eldridge turned and saw what was happening. Acting quickly, he untangled the reins from Henry's collar and helped Daisy back up onto her feet.

My pants were torn to shreds, as was my leg—there was blood everywhere—but by the mercy and grace of the Lord, not a bone had been broken.

I was generally an obedient child, but like all children I could be willful at times. It was on one of those occasions that I learned an important lesson about obedience and taking responsibility for one's actions.

I was about twelve years old at the time—this would have been around 1935—when my mother decided to travel to visit Grandmother Elmira in Alexandria, which was about seventy miles away. It was a good half-day's journey by train. Before leaving, she gave my father very explicit instructions regarding myself.

"Edmond," she said to Papa, "don't let this boy out of your sight. The only place you are to allow him to go is to his Grandmother Florestine's house—nowhere else."

Of course, my father promised Mama that her instructions would be followed to the letter.

The next day, I asked Papa if I could go visit Grandmother Florestine and my Aunt Christelia and my cousins Lincoln and Moses, who were living with her at the time. He said I could go, provided I kept Mama's wishes in mind.

Well, I hadn't been at Grandmother Florestine's house a few minutes when I suggested to my cousins that we go swimming in the bayou about a mile and a half into the woods. We sneaked off, going through all the tall weeds so no one could see us. We got to the water, stripped buck-born naked, and jumped in. We were having the time of our lives, when out of nowhere, Uncle John showed up in his wagon. There was no reason why he should have been passing by that way, because he lived clear on the other side of the bayou.

But there he was. He greeted us briefly, then drove on.

We sneaked back to Grandmother Florestine's house, and I returned home thinking I'd really put one over on Papa.

He was waiting for me on the front porch. "Where have you been, boy?" he demanded.

Innocently, I replied, "To Grandma's house."

Papa's gray eyes were smoldering with a hot, angry fire. "*Don't* you come lyin' to me, boy! Your Uncle John told me he *saw* you boys naked as jaybirds, splashin' 'round in the bayou!"

Before I could say anything, Papa grabbed a "young man peach-tree switch" he'd hidden on the porch, grabbed me, and gave me the whipping of my life.

You see, Uncle John had gone straight to Papa after he saw us boys where we weren't supposed to be. It was a lesson I never forgot, and it taught me something else—"it takes a village to raise a child." Back in those days, more families were extended—not like today, where the burden for raising children is laid on two—and more often, only one person. In fact, it takes not only a mother and a father, but uncles, aunts, grandparents, brothers, sisters, and cousins to do the job right. There's nothing "traditional" about a "nuclear" family, and we need to rectify that by taking an interest in our neighbors' children as well as our own.

Growing up, my cousins and I spent leisure time shooting marbles, playing ball, hunting, fishing, and doing what all boys do. We also did something a lot of boys don't do. At one point, my cousins Lincoln, Joseph, and Jacob and I formed a singing group. We sang hymns at the Truevine Baptist Church in four-part harmony and became quite the hit. We even wound up in a friendly competition — which we won — against a quartet from another church nearby.

I'll never forget that day. Afterward, during the social time, some of the girls from the other church came over to us and introduced themselves. The prettiest of them started in on what I think young people call "putting the moves" on me.

She did not mince words. Gazing into my eyes, she whispered, "Just being near you makes me feel like pitching a fog!"

Well, I being a healthy young buck of no little temptation... let me just say that we did have a heavy fog that night — and there was much dew on the grass the next day. To young people I say, pray unceasingly when you find yourselves tempted by the ways of the flesh. Pray to your Heavenly Father for the strength to resist seduction, for "broad is the path that leadeth to destruction."

Holidays

Christmas was the one day of the year to which we looked forward with greater anticipation than any other. There was always a special Christmas program at school that included the singing of Christmas songs and recitations.

At home, we would have a large tree with gifts under it. Mama would make a number of popcorn balls, each the size of a coconut and covered with sugar syrup.

Mama and my sisters would wash and clean the house so everything was sparkling clean. We butchered a hog a week or so before Christmas in order to have a fresh ham for dinner that day; Mama would bake cakes and pies of every kind, including coconut, chocolate, sweet potato, fig, peach preserve, and more.

On Christmas Eve, Mama would have us hang up our stockings on the mantel over the fireplace. She would then cut a slice of cake and set it on the table with a glass of table wine.

We children always got up early on Christmas Day and looked for presents left in our stockings. We usually received fruit, candy, and firecrackers; I got a cap pistol one year and usually received new clothing such as a new shirt, underdrawers, or trousers.

We always had a family prayer meeting on Christmas before breakfast, which featured real eggnog. You'd hear firecrackers all over the area on Christmas morning. It was a tradition for our family to visit all our aunts and uncles within walking distance—but not before we'd gone to see Grandmother Florestine first. Some years, we would have Christmas dinner there. Wherever we went, we were offered pie, cake, and table wine—one of the rare occasions we allowed ourselves to drink anything containing alcohol.

New Year's Eve was hardly less festive. We children were allowed to stay up past midnight, when everyone in the community would shoot Roman candles and light sparklers and firecrackers. Mama would serve a traditional midnight meal of real Cajun goose gumbo, along with hogshead cheese and all the trimmings.

These are some of my fondest childhood memories. But all things—especially childhood—must come to an end. The Lord put me on earth for a special purpose—which He was to reveal to me at a very early age.

Chapter II
Answering the Call

The Truevine Baptist Church was about two and a half miles from our home. Faith was always the center of our family life, and this was especially apparent on Sundays—for which we prepared on Saturday.

The Spiritual Life

Because the Lord's Day is one for rest and worship, my mother began cooking Sunday dinner on Saturday. We usually took baths on Saturday night before going to bed, heating water on the stove and using a large washtub (it's hard to imagine nowadays, but most folks don't realize that up until the middle of the twentieth century, very few American homes had indoor plumbing at all).

For as far back as I can remember, Sunday started with a family prayer meeting before breakfast. This always began with a reading from the Scripture, followed by song and prayer from my parents and closing with the Lord's Prayer. We then sat down to a hearty breakfast, after which we'd dress and leave for church.

Usually, we had Sunday School for a half hour before the worship service. On the first and third Sunday of every month, our pastor, the Reverend

James D. Smith, would conduct the service, and his wife would play for the hymn singing. Other Sundays were for what we called "Speaking Meeting," which today we call bearing one's testimony. Everyone in the church was expected to stand up before the congregation to bear witness of how he or she came to the Lord, then shake hands with all the deacons, who would be seated up front by the pulpit.

A testimony might go something like this: "Brothers and sisters, my determination is that since I have been converted, I treat everyone right... I'm neither tired nor worried... I aim to run on and see what the end's gonna be." After this, someone would lead off singing, "This little light of mine—I'm gonna let it shine..."

The first Sunday of every month was for Holy Communion and baptism. Whenever there were people desiring to be born again in Jesus, they would be taken to a pond there on the church grounds where the actual baptism would take place, accompanied by the deacons and the choir, who would be singing "Take Me To The Water." The whole congregation would stand by, singing and shouting their praises to the King of Kings. Afterwards, these new Christians were dried off and dressed, and then we would all reassemble to hear the Good News and partake in the Lord's Supper.

These are my most vivid childhood memories, and none stands out more than that of my own baptism.

Born Again

"Unless ye are born again of water and the Spirit, ye cannot enter the Kingdom of God." I was nine years old when I made the decision to give my life over to the Lord Jesus. It came one Sunday after Reverend Smith had preached a real hellfire-and-brimstone sermon, after which he extended the invitation to all who would to give their lives to Jesus.

I went right up and shook Reverend Smith's hand. But it wasn't that simple; anyone seeking baptism had to go before the deacons and answer questions about their conversion. If what you said was plausible, you were allowed to be baptized. If your answers did not meet their expectations, however, you were told to go and pray about it some more.

Imagine how I felt when my own Grandmother Florestine said, "He is not ready… he will have to go back and pray some more."

Naturally, I went back and sought the Lord's counsel in serious prayer, asking his forgiveness for my sinful pride and to be made a fit subject for His Heavenly Kingdom. The answer came to me in a vision; I saw myself being led to the pond to be baptized, and as I reached the pond, an Invisible Hand made the Sign of the Cross on the face of the waters.

When I spoke of this vision, it was assurance enough for the deacons and deaconesses—including my grandmother.

By the time of my baptism, the pond on our church grounds had dried up, so baptisms took place in a bayou about three or four miles from the church. It was here that I was born again of water and the Spirit, baptized by Reverend Smith and Uncle Leon, a large man and chairman of the deacons.

Uncle Leon was loved by most and respected by all; when the congregation got too noisy, he would simply stand, raising his hands and say, "My brothers and sisters, you are too noisy…remember you are in the HOUSE OF THE LORD." Within seconds, the noise would die down and we could commence with the service.

School Days

Faith was the center of our lives, but even as Children of God we must live in and as part of the world. A child's secular education is as important in many ways as his Gospel schooling, and it was certainly true in my case.

Not all lessons were learned in school, however. When we were old enough, my cousins Lincoln and Moses and I would earn money by splitting rails and cording up firewood. Pay was as much as a dollar a day, which was quite a bit for a young black man back then.

You may recall me saying that back in those days in Louisiana, race was complicated, and you could be judged not only on the basis of being "black" or "white," but if you had any African ancestry at all, how light or dark you were. One day, the three of us went to the commissary store to collect our pay. The clerk looked at me first.

"What's your name, boy?"

"Samuel Joubert," I answered.

He nodded and said, "I know him." Then he looked at my cousin Lincoln, who'd inherited our Grandmother Florestine's light skin and blue eyes. "And who are you?"

"Lincoln Thomas, sir."

Next, he looked over at my cousin Moses, who took after his father—as dark-skinned as an Ashanti or Yoruban prince. "What's your name, boy?"

"I'm Moses Thomas, sir."

That clerk looked at my two cousins. "You boys have the same father?" he asked, as though not quite believing it.

Moses spoke up. "Yes, sir."

The clerk took a long look at both of them. He chuckled, shook his head and said, "Your daddy musta been born on the dark side o' the moon, eh, boy?"

It was obviously an issue for him, which was hard for me to understand. I loved both my cousins equally—the fact that one of them was dark-skinned and the other light-skinned never occurred to me.

Since that time, I have only judged men or women by what is in their hearts and by their actions. The color of their skin says nothing about who they are in the eyes of the Lord. It is how I have always lived my life.

In our community, blacks had a wooden schoolhouse with two classrooms (one for grades one through three and the other for grades four through seven), a kitchen, and a coatroom. Each classroom had a potbellied stove for heat in the winter. It was the only school for blacks for miles around—and the only way to get there was to walk.

In contrast, the white children had an elementary school as well as a high school, both constructed with brick. Those white students who did not live within walking distance got to ride the school bus. If the bus passed black children walking to their school, they had to move into the ditch. If they got splattered with dust or mud, the white children would laugh as though it were the funniest thing they'd ever seen.

White students were given new books. After they'd been used for a few years, they would be replaced, and we would get the old ones.

Wherever you went in those days in the South, bus stations, railroad deports, or anywhere else, everything was segregated—there were separate waiting rooms for blacks and whites, separate rest rooms, and even drinking fountains marked "white" and "colored."

Even health care was a race issue. There were no black doctors in our community, and even the waiting rooms in clinics were separate. It didn't matter when you showed up or when your appointment was (if you had one): if you were black, you had to wait until all the white patients had been seen. If you showed up when the office opened, and the doctor had white patients, you had to wait all day. And if you hadn't been seen by closing time, well, too bad—you had to come back the next day.

It didn't stop there. Our family raised cotton, and we'd wind up with five or six bales every year. On many occasions I went with my father to the cotton gin, where the seed was separated from the bale itself. When the bale was weighed, I'd stand next to Papa and watch the white man steal from him by tilting the scale.

"Papa, that scale ain't balanced!" I'd whisper.

Despite the fact that he was being cheated, he'd not say a word. Who was a black farmer going to complain to?

How easy it would have been to become angry, bitter, and hate-filled like some of our people did up North. Were it not for the power of the Lord within me, I might have become as reactionary as those who raised fists and started riots in cities like Detroit and Los Angeles. It is not my place to judge them — but I thank the Lord that I was guided on to a different path.

The Making of an Orator

The 4-H Club has always been a great help to those of us who have ever worked tilling the land and raising livestock. When I was a boy, one Mr. Leon Robinson was the 4-H Club County Agent for those of us in St. Landry Parish.

Mr. Robinson was to play a key role in my early life. Not only did I learn how to graft fruit trees and rotate the soil, as well as many other ways to improve our crop yields, I got many learning opportunities outside of St. Landry's thanks to my association with him. Every summer, I went with Mr. Robinson to the annual meeting of the Louisiana State 4-H at Southern University in Scotlandville, where short courses in agriculture were offered.

What was most significant about that first summer at Southern University, however, was that it marked the beginning of my career as a public speaker.

Strangely, this came about not because I was especially good at giving speeches, but because I was popular with the girls. It so happened that one of the girls that summer — this was 1937 — put my name up for nomination to one of the state 4-H offices. To make a long story short, I was duly elected as the President of the Louisiana State 4-H. It was the first of the many times I would give a public address, as short as it was: "I am happy to be here... I believe the influence I will have as your President will allow me to do more helpful things in the community."

I wound up serving as state president for the next three years. As I traveled around the state with Mr. Robinson, I gave addresses at many schools and colleges, as well as the state 4-H Club Camp in Monroe, Louisiana. There, I spoke before an educated audience of county agents from all over Louisiana — including the state agent, Mr. T. J. Jordan.

I realized what an impression I had made later that evening as I was getting ready to turn in for the night. All the girls and boys who attended the camp slept in bunk beds in a large dormitory. I was getting ready to lie down in my bunk when Mr. Jordan came walking through and saw me.

"This is where they put you?" he asked.

I nodded. "Yes, sir!"

He shook his head. "This will never do," he said. He motioned me to come with him and bring my suitcase. As we walked, he said, "The State 4-H Club President will not sleep on a bunk bed."

I was housed in one of the best cabins on the site, with a room and a bath — a *bath* — all to myself.

That summer, at the short course at Southern University, I gave the following speech:

"As workers together in the industry of agriculture, producing the various commodities we all need, I suggest that we stop crying *'give me!'* or *'help me!'* while setting our buckets down on the sea of time… let us not be afraid to work harder where we are, and we will be able to come up with our buckets full of the commodities we need."

But all this was only preparation for my true calling, which I was soon to hear.

Chapter III
Path to the Pulpit

As far back as I can remember, I knew I was called to the pulpit—the only question was when I would begin.

It was a cold day in the early winter of 1938. This was hog butchering time, so Mama and Papa had gone up to the home of one of my aunts to help lay in our winter's supply of ham and bacon. I had other plans that Saturday, however.

I washed up, put on my Sunday-go-to-meeting clothes, and walked the two and a half miles to the Truevine Baptist Church. Our pastor had recently passed on to his reward, and the deacons were meeting in a small room on one side of the pulpit.

I arrived just as my Uncle Leon was about to convene the meeting. When I announced that I wanted to address the deacons, I was asked to wait in the other room.

After what seemed like hours, I heard Uncle Leon leading the deacons in their closing prayer. As they stirred to leave, I heard my uncle say, "Oh, yes—before we close, let's find out what that boy wants." He came into the other room on the other side of the pulpit where I sat waiting and motioned for me to come.

I was a little nervous standing there in front of the Council of Deacons like that when then asked me why I had come. I cleared my throat and said, "I am called to preach—and I have come to make it known and hopefully be given a chance."

They asked me a number of questions, and evidently my answers were convincing; they agreed to hear me right then and there. My theme for that first sermon was John the Baptist. I began: "In those days, John the Baptist came preaching in the wilderness of Judah..."

I'll never forget that first sermon. When I finished, my Aunt Clementine, who was one of the deacons, embraced me and said, "Son... one day you will be a great preacher. I will be praying for you."

When my older brother Eldridge, who was already a preacher, got word of it, he was not nearly as impressed. He complained to Mama, "That boy is just trying to imitate me!" He changed his tune when he heard me, though. After listening to one of my sermons, he said, "I take back all I said... that boy really *is* called to preach!"

A Preacher's Education

I was sixteen years old at the time, and attending high school over in Opelousas, about five miles away. It was during this time that I became acquainted with the pastor of the Little Zion Baptist Church, Dr. L. C. Simon. Dr. Simon was not only one of the leading pastors in the state of Louisiana, he was also a trustee of Leland College and a respected scholar as well as the instructor for the Louisiana State Convention Ministers' Seminar.

One day, Dr. Simon said to me, "Brother Joubert, I

am preaching at a Baptist Church here in town on the occasion of the unveiling of the new pulpit this Friday night. I wish you to accompany me." Naturally, I could not refuse this request—not only would I get to hear Dr. Simon preach, but I'd witness the unveiling ceremony—something I'd not heard of before. But that was not the biggest surprise I was to receive.

When we arrived at the church that evening, I met the new pastor, whom I remembered seeing before. We sat in his office and chatted until it was time to begin the service. As we left the pastor's study, we encountered Dr. Simon, who announced to the pastor, "By the way, I am not delivering the sermon this evening." He indicated me. "This young man will preach tonight."

You can imagine how frightened I was—and seeing a number of my classmates sitting out there in the congregation did not make me feel any less apprehensive.

For better or worse, I had memorized my "trial sermon"—which consisted of the entire third chapter of the Gospel According to Saint Matthew. I recited it word for word, raising my voice for the climax as I reached the end.

On the way home, I asked Dr. Simon what he thought of the message. "It was O.K.," he said.

A few days later, however, he called me into his study. "Sit down, Brother Joubert," he said. I did so. He started pacing. "Now you listen to me," he said sternly, "In the first place, that 'sermon' last Friday night was *not* preaching. What you did was a loud reading." He let that sink in, then explained: "Preaching is when you take a passage from the scripture, then explain that text to the congregation by comparing it to other passages, teaching them how to apply the message… what it means to one's everyday living with the emphasis on the fact that salvation is in Christ."

I knew of course that in order to be saved, one must accept Jesus Christ as his or her personal savior. What I had failed to do was use the scripture to illustrate this fundamental tenet of our faith. This was my first lesson in how to preach a sermon.

I confess however that I was as yet untempered. Like so many young men, I was prideful, arrogant, and full of myself. Sometime later, Dr. Simon requested that I accompany him and some of his colleagues to a meeting of a district association up in Garland, about ten miles north of Opelousas. I replied that I was not interesting in attending their meeting because there was nothing I could learn from those ignorant preachers.

I'll never forget the look in Dr. Simon's eyes when he looked at me. You would have thought I'd thrown boiling water in his face. In a low voice, he said, "Young man… don't you *ever* let me hear you speak that way about God's People again. When and wherever men and women of God meet there is *always* something you can learn and with which you can be helped."

Needless to say, I accompanied Dr. Simon to that meeting—at which I was greatly inspired and helped.

Tempering

During my training in Opelousas, I attended worship services at the Little Zion Baptist Church where many of the local schoolteachers also came to worship. Dr. Simon was kind enough to have me preach one Sunday morning. As luck would have it, my English teacher was in the congregation that day to hear my sermon.

A few days later, she proceeded to critique my message in front of the entire class. "Mr. Joubert's pose and diction were excellent," she concluded, adding, "his message was interesting, and his delivery was up to par." But then she said, "I was however disappointed, because he did not use a manuscript."

That made *me* disappointed, because I had put great effort into memorizing what I had planned to say that morning. Our teacher explained: "I expect the preacher to have a manuscript up there on the pulpit even if he doesn't use it, because it demonstrates that he did make some preparation."

Since that time, I have always kept a manuscript with me on the pulpit.

More Lessons

During my freshman year I lived in a room located in a black man's mansion owned by some relatives. I shared the room with my cousin Cephas; our landlord, Mr. Desotel, was a tall, heavily-build mulatto who was very smart and very thrifty, and he would tell long jokes that would make you laugh until you almost needed stitches.

The next year I made arrangements to stay in the home of my mentor, Dr. Simon. He'd asked, "Boy, can you cook?"

I replied, "Oh, yes." I wasn't lying—even though I'd never cooked in my life. It was just that I'd seen Mama make biscuits so often, I really thought I could do as well.

Dr. Simon nodded. "Your stay will be determined by how well you can cook," he informed me.

The first several weeks I was living there, Dr. Simon prepared breakfast. Then one day, he placed all the ingredients on the table and announced, "From now on, Brother Joubert, you will prepare your own breakfast as well as mine."

I tried—but I did not even get to first base. I'd never even boiled an egg growing up—Mama and my oldest sister Clara Eulalee had done all the cooking in our home.

Nonetheless, it came as a shock when Dr. Simon sat me down one morning. "Boy," he admonished, "you *can't cook!* You *lied* to me!" There was nothing I could say. He continued: "I have enough trouble cooking for you and looking out for your welfare, boy. You will have to find somewhere else to stay."

I was crushed—and a little desperate, because all the boarding houses for students in the community were filled by that time. In my naiveté, I thought just because he was a preacher and I was a preacher-in-training, he'd somehow let me slide.

I pleaded with Dr. Simon to let me stay, but he was adamant. "I am doing this for your own good, boy."

Looking at the possibility of sleeping on a park

bench, I turned to the Lord for help. By His Grace, an opening came.

A queen of a woman owned a restaurant that happened to have some rooms upstairs—and Hallelujah! She had a vacancy! It worked out very well not only for me, but for her as well. You remember that I was very popular with the young ladies. Well, as it turned out, the girls at school found out I was taking my noontime meal at the restaurant, so they came flocking—and the other boys came following the girls. As a result, my landlady's restaurant did very well.

We do not always know His greater purposes.

I learned that when you live right, pray constantly, and keep faith with the Lord, He will not only see you through your dark moments, but will bring sunshine into your life with even greater blessing than you imagined.

Incidentally, despite the unpleasantness, my relationship with Dr. Simon never changed, and we remained the closest of friends until his passing many years later.

Government Helps People Help Themselves

These days it's popular to bash our nation's government, but back then during the Great Depression, it was a good thing. President Roosevelt was as flawed as any man, but he was still a great leader who loved, served, and cared for the people of this country.

I know this firsthand, because I was a beneficiary of one of President Roosevelt's programs. While I attended the Opelousas school, I would receive a check from a government program called the National Recovery Act. The purpose was to facilitate the nation's return to prosperity by investing in people—particularly students like me.

I received between seven and nine dollars a month, which was a fair amount in those days. In exchange, we would work maintaining the school building—cleaning, running the furnace on cold days, keeping everything operating, and the like. Ultimately, the principal put me in charge as a crew supervisor. We were responsible for all the janitorial work that needed doing as well as keeping the boiler room in order and supplied with fuel.

On some occasions when one of my teachers had to leave the room during class, I would often be asked to take charge until he or she returned. Somehow, I was always able to maintain proper discipline and decorum until the teacher returned.

Moving On

As I look back on nearly nine decades of my life on this planet, I can almost literally see the Almighty Hand of God guiding, directing, and protecting me. I remember vividly that Sunday morning in December of 1938 when his Hand changed my direction and got me headed from where I was going to His destination.

My cousins Lincoln and Matthew had enrolled in the Opelousas school at the beginning of that academic year. When classes ended for the Christmas holiday recess, we headed home to Grand Prairie. Lincoln and I considered going over to Jeanerette about fifty miles southeast on US Highway 90, where the sugar cane growers were paying $1.25 per day plus room and board. The plan was to spend Christmas recess there earning a few extra dollars to help defray our school expenses.

I got home on Saturday and asked Mama if I could go cane cutting. At first she refused, but the next morning before sunrise, I overheard her talking to Papa.

"Maybe we should let Bertie go," I heard her say.

I jumped out of bed and ran into the front room. "Mama, did I hear you say I could go?"

"Well, Bertie, I don't think—"

"But I heard you say I could go!"

She looked at me a moment, then said, "All right, Bertie."

In less than ten minutes, I was dressed, out the door, and running to Aunt Christelia's house to give Lincoln the news. His parents had given their consent as well; after breakfast, Lincoln threw his clothes into a bundle, and we started out for Washington, ten miles away, where we hoped to catch a ride on a truck heading for Jeanerette.

We were almost to Washington when we met Brother Rose, an elderly member of the Truevine Baptist Church, out driving in his horse-drawn buggy. He stopped. "So where are you boys headed?"

We told him of our plans to work the cane fields in Jeanerette. He nodded, then said, "My son Joshua is working a government job up in Alexandria—pays eight dollars an hour."

That was a fabulous sum in those days when a bank teller's salary was around one hundred dollars a month. Eight dollars an *hour*? That's more than we'd get in a whole *week* in the cane fields (which for those of you who don't know, is strenuous and brutal physical labor).

We thanked Brother Rose for the information as he went on his way. I then turned to my cousin. "What do you think?" I asked.

"What do *you* think?"

"I think we ought to go to Alexandria," I replied.

He grinned. "Well—let's go!"

Alexandria was as far away as Jeanerette, but in the opposite direction—north. Fortunately, we found a man with a truck in Washington who was heading in that direction and agreed to allow us to ride with him.

We got to Alexandria about one in the afternoon. We found out that the government work was at an aircraft and munitions assembly plant (Pearl Harbor was three years in the future, but there were people in President Roosevelt's Administration who could see what was coming). We were directed to go to the local Methodist Church on Murray Street. When we got there, we found *hundreds* of people milling around, waiting.

We hung out there until sundown—to no avail. After dark, we went over to the "colored area" on Lee Street and sat in a cafe there until they put us out. We went to another and stayed until *it* closed, and so forth—and eventually wound up spending the night on some park benches.

We returned to the Murray Street Methodist

Church the next day and found the same crowd standing there in hopes of securing employment. Before long, a gentleman came forward and asked, "Is there a boy here under eighteen who wants a job?"

Before he could finish, my hand was in the air. "I'll take it!" I said quickly. He handed me a card with the name and address of a nearby establishment.

I soon found the place—a cafe that was looking for a dishwasher. They hired me right then and there, and I was informed that my shift would be from 6 p.m. to 2 a.m.

Lincoln was unable to find a job and went home to Grand Prairie.

As I was trying to figure out where I would stay while in Alexandria, it occurred to me that my Grandmother Elmira lived nearby as did my oldest sister Clara and my Aunt Virginia, who had recently separated from her husband. Of course, they were happy to have me there while I worked at the cafe.

The job at the cafe and my living arrangement with my extended family members worked out so well that after a week, I concluded that I should make my move to Alexandria permanent. Grandmother Elmira, Aunt Virginia, and my sister Clara were all very much in favor of this idea.

When I went to the local high school and approached the principal, Mr. David Iles, on the possibility of enrollment, he was very cordial. "No problem," he assured me after hearing what I had to say. "We'll be happy to have you."

Arranging to take a few days off from my dishwashing job, I returned to Grand Prairie and told

Mama and Papa what I had in mind. They gladly gave me their blessing.

In fact, the only opposition I received was from the principal of the Opelousas school. He seemed almost hurt when he said, "Aren't you doing well here? You're one of our model students, and we have high hopes and plans for you."

Nonetheless, I was determined to follow through. Reluctantly, he said, "Very well… I'll see your transcript is sent to Peabody High School." Looking at me, he laid a hand on my shoulder as he said, "You can always come back here if you change your mind."

The next day found me, my suitcases, and my books aboard a Greyhound bus heading north to Alexandria.

Once I had settled in with my extended family, my first step was (of course!) to find a church home. My grandmother, aunt, and sister were members of the Rose of Sharon Baptist Church, the pastor of which was the Reverend J. W. White. Reverend White had not only baptized my mother as a girl but had also performed the wedding ceremony when she married Papa. It was almost a foregone conclusion that I would be accepted as a member once Reverend White learned that I was my mother's son.

Moving Up

I worked at the Post Office Cafe for some time, but I finally realized that working from 6 p.m. to 2 a.m. was starting to take its toll on my health and my academic performance. I rarely got home before 2:30 or

3:00, which gave me four hours for sleep; I needed two more hours to get up, get breakfast, and walk to school in order to be there for the start of classes at nine, which lasted until around 3:30—giving me just enough time to get home, get changed, have some supper and report to the cafe.

This schedule gave me a total of thirty minutes a day for study and class work.

I found it increasingly difficult to stay awake in class and get assignments completed and turned in on time. To top it off, I was having difficulty with my mathematics teacher. He was not from southern Louisiana; he had an odd accent that made it difficult to understand when he was speaking. When lecturing, he would provide one example on the chalkboard, and those who did not understand it the first time were out of luck. In addition, anytime I raised my hand to ask a question, I was ignored.

Some help came through an acquaintance I'd made earlier through my 4-H Club activities. During my time at Grambling College, I met a charming young lady named Tena Jones, with whom I had kept in touch by mail. It so happened that two of my classmates in that math course were Tena's sisters, and when they realized who I was, they were only too pleased to do some of my assignments for me.

It was the Grace of God, however, that ultimately came to my rescue. It happened when Principal Iles asked me to meet with some members of the faculty and the student council. As it turned out, my math teacher was the liaison between the faculty and the student council. That day, Principal Iles recommended me for Student Council President, an office to which I was duly elected upon that recommendation.

As he did with pharaoh for the Children of Israel, the Lord softened my math teacher's heart toward me. From then on, my questions were answered and explanations made thoroughly—and my marks in mathematics returned to their usual high level.

Nonetheless, I knew I had to find some other employment that would allow me more time for study, school work, and taking care of my health—meaning more sleep.

I quit my job at the cafe and went looking. I stopped by a department store on Front Street and asked if they needed a porter.

The white man to whom I spoke was very kind and helpful, but told me they had all the help they needed. However, the hotel a few doors down had recently undergone a change of ownership.

He said to me, "Go over there and tell the new owner that you heard he needed a porter. Don't tell him who sent you, just say you heard he needed some extra help."

I did exactly as he told me. Without delay I went and spoke to the new owner of the hotel. He had just moved up from New Orleans and invested in the place because the Army had established three or four bases nearby—and there'd be a lot of soldiers who'd be coming into town on three-day passes needing a place to stay.

The owner looked at me and said, "I don't need another porter today. Come back day after tomorrow."

I returned the second day right after school. He

was surprised to see me. He looked me over and said, "I really don't need another porter — but since you did come back, I'll give you a try."

The hotel was undergoing renovation at the time; walls needed to be painted in the main halls as well as the rooms. The owner showed me how to mix the paint and how to use the brush, working alongside me until he was sure I'd gotten the hang of it.

Over the coming weeks, I did just about anything that needed doing; I swept and mopped, cleaned toilets, and more. As the renovation project was winding down, I did something that changed the owner's attitude towards me completely.

When you live on the farm, you learn how to work hard and fast; cotton must be harvested before the rains come, livestock must be fed on schedule and quickly, cows must be milked every day in a short amount of time, and broken fences and gates must be mended before animals have a chance to wander off into the bayou and turn into 'gator feed. I'd learned much that I could apply to my new situation.

One night, the hotel owner met me when I arrived at 6 p.m. and showed me to a few rooms that had yet to be painted. He gave me the paint, brushes, and turpentine then went back to his office, leaving me alone — no supervision, no other help.

It was just what I wanted. I used the techniques I'd learned growing up on the farm to complete the painting in less than half the time it would have normally taken — including going back over everything and making certain there were no spots or places left undone.

When I told the owner I'd finished, he looked at me and said, "Sam, don't you play games with me—there's no way you could have finished all that unless you did a half-a**ed job!"

He came and checked it thoroughly—and was completely overwhelmed. Although my shift was not over, he turned to me and said, "Go on home, son—you've done your work for tonight."

The next day when I reported for work, he handed me a clean white jacket with the name of the hotel printed on it. "Sam," he said, "from now on you let the other fellows do the mopping and cleaning the toilets. You'll work behind the desk and do other chores as I deem necessary." He also pointed out a door across the hall from the desk, which led to a special suite reserved for his wife and daughter when they would come up from New Orleans to visit. Then he showed me a three-foot flat iron he kept hidden under the desk. "Now," he said, "your main job is to check in our guests, assign them rooms and collect money." Then, holding up the iron and pointing to the door, he said, "If you ever see anyone heading toward that door other than myself, you are to whack them with this and call the police. You understand, Samuel?"

I nodded.

Thanks be to God, I never had to perform that duty during my tenure there.

There was another side to this man, however. Before I started my new duties, he said, "Sam, remember that we are in business to make money—and half a loaf is sometimes better than none. Our rooms let for three dollars a night, but if someone comes in and says they don't have that much, you tell 'im to wait, 'cause you might have a room you can give 'im for two dollars. Go up to the same room you were going to give 'im, come back, and tell 'im you've arranged it. We never want to turn away a paying customer if they can pay anything at all, you understand?"

This white Frenchman from New Orleans was one of the kindest men I ever knew, and I remember him with great affection. One time, when he paid me for my week's labors, he said, "Sam, I usually don't shake hands with coloreds, but in your case I will make an exception." It occurred to me as he shook my hand that day that this was perhaps insulting on one level—but a man is the product of his upbringing, and I understood that he was trying to reach out as best he could.

My working hours were usually from six to ten at night, after which I was to be relieved by a man named Winters. He had a habit of not showing up on occasion, however. On those nights, I was allowed to go home, get my schoolbooks and return to the hotel. During the night shift, I had plenty of time to study and finish class assignments.

The job also had its privileges. Some nights around midnight, the boss would get hungry and send me over to this restaurant over on Third Street, about four blocks from the hotel. As you probably know, back in those days, such restaurants were "Whites Only." Being "colored," I would not normally be allowed to enter such a restaurant through the front door, or even eat there. This kind of discrimination was codified into law in the South at that time.

However, that white jacket was my passport. As a staff member of one of Alexandria's better hotels, I was allowed to enter in the front, present the *maitre'd* with a note indicating what my employer wanted to eat, and in short order I was presented with a sandwich and a bottle of beer to take back to the hotel.

Jim Crow laws had their exceptions depending on just how liberal a white person's attitudes were and how much power or influence he had.

A Dutiful Son

As I enjoyed my relative prosperity in Alexandria, I could never forget Mama and Papa—and especially how Papa was in perpetual debt to the commissary store. I vowed that I would free Papa from those chains. I opened an account at a bank in Alexandria, and over the next year was able to save almost three hundred dollars—more enough to pay off my father's account at the commissary store.

The day I was back in Grand Prairie, I dressed in my finest suit, shined my shoes, and drove over to the store with Papa.

All eyes were on me when Papa and I walked into that store, because none of them had ever seen a well-dressed black man before. I went up to one of the partners who was standing behind the counter. I asked him how much my father owed him. With trembling hands, he pulled out a ledger, turned the pages to my father's name and said, "One hundred and fifty-one dollars even."

I pulled out my wallet and counted out the money,

then asked for a receipt. As he wrote it, the old man turned to my father and said, "You should be proud of your son… what he has done is most unusual."

On the way home, I said to Papa, "If you ever get in a situation in which you are short on funds, let me know."

Yes, life in Alexandria was good — but there were certain facts of life, and the central fact of my life was my being a person of African ancestry, living in a hostile society dominated by people whose ancestors had brought my ancestors to this country against our will — and now held that against us.

I was to be reminded of this fact again and again in the coming years.

Chapter IV
The Facts of Life

I do not pretend to know what the experience of my black brothers in the north was like during the years that we in the South suffered under the harsh inequities of Jim Crow. Certainly there was injustice for blacks throughout the country; before the courts of law, a white man's prank was all-too-often a black man's felony.

I do know that the Southern white man's hatred and contempt for his black brother was expressed far more blatantly in the South. For example, I know of no lynchings that took place in the North; there were neighborhoods in Northern cities where black people could not live and public places into which they could not go, but as far as I know, such discrimination was not codified into law as it was in the South. Prejudice and bigotry among northern whites was more subtle, more "beneath the surface," so to speak, whereas in the South bigotry was expressed openly and was even considered socially acceptable.

Given these facts, I wonder why, when the inevitable backlash came starting in the 1950s and '60s, the reactions among Southern blacks was so centered on peace and reconciliation, whereas up north, too many of our black brothers expressed rage through violence. The "black power," hate-fueled anger of Stokely Carmichael and Malcolm X was a product of northern cities. The Reverend Martin Luther King on the other hand was a product of the rural South.

My reactions to the injustices I suffered as a black man in the South are more like those of the late Reverend King; I cannot and will not hold hatred for any man any more than did our Lord Jesus when he said, "Forgive them, Father, for they know not what they do."

I must believe that the behavior of whites toward their black brethren was born of fear and ignorance rather than purposeful evil (except insofar as we have all fallen short of the glory of God). Nonetheless, my experiences as a black man in the South during the days of Jim Crow are part of what I am—and they are part of our shared history. I would do the reader an injustice if I did not relate some of the events of those days.

Betrayal

After school was out for the summer—this was 1940—I got a job working for one of Alexandria's wealthiest and most prominent families, the Skyles. Fortunately for me, Mrs. Skyles, a tall, stately woman, was as close as anyone came in those days to a Southern liberal, and her husband—who was shorter that his wife—was greatly influenced by her views. Their son was a tall, handsome fellow to whom much authority was given in matters of running the family business.

I was hired by the Skyles family to work on the renovation of a two story building they owned that was located on Third Street. It was about half a block long and at least forty feet wide. The upper floor had a large, empty space that was to be made into a ballroom known as the "Skyles Roof Garden." By the time the renovation was completed, the Skyles Roof Garden had all the amenities in addition to the dance floor; there was a kitchen and dining area, a cloakroom, restrooms with running water, and the business office.

The Grand Opening was scheduled for a Saturday night. I was issued a white jacket and put in charge of the cloakroom. All the waiters were black as well. The entire operation was managed and overseen by young Mr. Skyles; he issued the orders, and we carried them out.

I am proud to say that during my entire tenure as check boy, no article was ever misplaced nor lost. I developed a unique method of placing hats, coats and other articles in a systematic way—and it worked like a charm.

Most of our patrons were servicemen from up North stationed at one of the nearby bases who came in with their girlfriends. On occasion, they would stop and chat with me. I would often say something complimentary; for example, referring to a serviceman's girlfriend, I might say, "Man, you sure know how to pick 'em!" and to him I'd say, "and that uniform looks like it was tailor made for you!" It worked; when I returned their article, I was invariably given a good tip.

Once I had the checkroom routine established, Mr. Skyles turned it over to two white girls and moved me out to the floor waiting tables. I made even better tips as a waiter; it didn't take me long to learn the ropes. Once I had learned the job, I was able to move faster than the other waiters who'd been at it longer than I, and I always brought customers' orders to their table with a broad smile and a kind word.

The winds of war were blowing even then, and young Mr. Skyles joined the increasing number of men who were signing up for military service. After he left for basic training, the elder Mr. Skyles had a vacancy to fill—"and there arose in Egypt a new pharaoh who knew Joseph not."

For whatever reason, the new manager did not like me. The other waiters knew I was a young preacher, as did young Mr. Skyles; when he had been in charge, he had been very understanding and was gracious enough to allow me Sundays off.

That first Saturday night working under the new manager, I was preparing to leave when he confronted me.

"I've been told that you haven't been coming in Sunday morning to help the other waiters clean up from Saturday night," he said.

I replied, "When Mr. Skyles hired me he knew I was a preacher and I would not be required to work on Sundays."

The new manager snapped, "*I'm* in charge now, boy—and I'm telling you that you must work on Sunday along with the rest of waiters."

I realized that I had been betrayed by my own brothers—the other waiters who resented the fact that I got Sundays off. I said, "I'm sorry, but I will not come into work on the Sabbath Day."

"Then your services are no longer required."

"Okay," I said, and I walked out.

Betrayal by my own was an experience that, as you can surely imagine, I'd have certainly preferred not to have had. But the Lord presents us what we need to learn, and from this betrayal I learned the importance of remaining true and maintaining integrity.

Compassion

My next job was at a soft drink bottling plant. The process of brewing and bottling was like an assembly line; there were three stations on the main floor. Each of these were manned by a single employee on a rotating manner; the man at Station 1 would work there for thirty minutes before moving on to Station 2, at which time the one at Station 2 moved to 3, and the one at Station 3 relieved the man at Station 3.

Station 1 was where bottles were thoroughly washed before being placed upright on a conveyor belt about one foot apart. At Station 2, bottles were inspected for cleanliness; the employee sat on a high chair and looked at each bottle, through which a bright light was shone. If there were any particles or other signs that the bottle was not spotless, the bottle was removed from the conveyor belt. Station 3 was where the bottles were filled, capped, and placed by hand into cases, which in turn were placed on a ramp with rollers that carried them down into the basement.

I was taking my turn at Station 2—the inspection station—one hot day. I had not slept well the night before, and the heat caused me to doze off.

Suddenly, I felt a tap on my shoulder. I jerked awake.

It was the plant supervisor, Mr. Joddie.

Mr. Joddie was pointing to a bottle that had passed in front of the inspection light with a long stick in it.

I'm going to get sacked right here and now, I thought.

Instead, Mr. Joddie—who had put the stick in the bottle to trick me—just laughed it off. "Stay awake, Sam!" he chuckled.

Thanks be to God that not all white people are bigots. On my last day at the bottling plant, Mr. Joddie and my co-workers expressed their sorrow in seeing me go, but they wished me well.

Deception

The reason I left my job at the bottling plant was because I had qualified for a job at a veteran's hospital a few miles outside of town. In order to qualify, one had to pass an examination, which I had successfully passed a few weeks earlier.

At that place and time, the highest paying occupations for most blacks were that of railroad porter and working at a veteran's hospital; only professionals such as teachers, lawyers, and doctors earned more.

I was hired as a dishwasher. I acquitted myself well; when my probationary period was over, I was promoted and put on the swing shift. The job, which I did with one other person, was to make sure that each patient got the correct meal according to his dietary needs. We had to place a label on each tray with the name of the patient and the type of diet.

The Facts of Life

My co-workers (a black man in the afternoon and a white man in the evening) and I did this for every tray at every mealtime. Both of the men I worked with said they had never worked with a better partner. There were never any complaints from the head nurse, ward supervisors, or the patients.

I was also the youngest black employee at the hospital.

I was different than the other black employees at the hospital, who were older and less educated. During my lunch break, while the older men would be smoking, taking a drink, and chewing the fat, I would go to the hospital library and spend my time with a good book. I was well dressed, well groomed, and spoke excellent Standard English.

Apparently, I did not fit the white Establishment's expectations of the shuffling, subservient old Negro. I was therefore a threat to the *status quo*.

Almost overnight, my supervisor began finding fault with everything I did. Neither of my co-workers could understand her treatment of me. The white man, Maurice, said to me, "Sam, I don't understand why she keeps picking on you. Your work is perfect."

And it was.

Eventually, this supervisor—a nurse of short stature—began to hate my very presence. The problem was that mine was a civil service position, so I could not be fired without demonstrated cause—and even if there was, I was legally entitled to a hearing.

Nonetheless, the personnel department had decided that I had to go—there was no place at that hospital for an "uppity Negro" who obviously didn't know his place! Unfortunately for them, my work was excellent, and my co-workers would attest to this fact.

One day, I was called to the office to sign the payroll. There was nothing unusual about this; whenever we were paid, we were required to sign for it. I'd done it so often that I didn't even think about it. I didn't even bother to check and *read* what I was signing anymore.

It's what they were counting on. The nurse at the window that day put out a piece of paper and said, "Sign here, please." I signed on the dotted line as usual—and I will never forget the heartless smirk on that woman's face when she looked up at me and said, "Your resignation has been accepted!"

I'd been tricked into signing my own resignation!

They meant it for evil… but the Lord turned it around for good. In His infinite wisdom, He knew that the longer I stayed on at the hospital, the more difficult it would be for me to return to my studies. It was necessary to prepare myself academically so I could carry out the work of the ministry more efficiently.

The Lord had decided it was time for me to go back to school.

CHAPTER V
PATHS AND PITFALLS

I was given license to preach at the Truevine Baptist Church under the leadership of the Reverend Matthew Antoine on the last day of February of 1939. During my time in Alexandria, I was ordained to preach at the Rose of Sharon Baptist Church. I had a ways to go, however, before I would be qualified to lead my own flock.

The Making of a Shepherd

Aside from Pastor Reverend White and myself, there were two ministers—middle-aged men who were also members of the church. These two men were "local," or associate, preachers. They were licensed to preach, but did not have the formal training and preparation required of a full pastor. They could nonetheless be ambitious.

It is not a good thing to be ambitious without having credentials or a portfolio. Overly ambitious associate preachers are known to sometimes join forces with disgruntled church officers and deacons in order to undermine pastoral authority. I was young and in school, and did my best to support Pastor White. After we had worked together for a year, he came to know that I was honest, loyal, and dependable; I would not attempt to undermine his relationship with the congregation in any way.

It was for this reason that he took me on as his son in the ministry. Pastor White was no longer young, and he was in need of an ordained minister to assist him. Some of the officers and other members of the church suggested to him that I be ordained for this purpose.

Although he initially resisted the idea, Pastor White decided to set a date for my examination for ordination. All he said to me was, "Son... prepare yourself for examination." He did not suggest a tutor, nor did he tutor me; he simply left me to study and prepare on my own.

During my time at Rose of Sharon, there was an elderly member of our congregation who took a special interest in me—a woman and a well-trained Bible scholar, as it turned out. She was of invaluable help to me in assembling my personal library. Among the books she recommended included the *New Chain Reference Bible*, a complete concordance to the Holy Scriptures of the old and new Testaments, a Bible commentary, and a Bible dictionary. These titles, she told me would serve as the basic working tools for the ministry.

Of course I immediately had added these titles to my library. Later, Pastor White had occasion to come by and visit my grandmother, where he saw my library of religious books. He was amazed.

In retrospect, I suppose my pastor assumed that with my schooling and such a library. I did not need to be tutored. I also felt that I was prepared for what was coming—but I was in for a real surprise.

As I prepared myself to serve the Kingdom, there

were nonetheless worldly matters to attend to. By this time, the nation was at war, and everyone was expected to do his or her part.

I had secured a job at Camp Claiborne in the hospital as an orderly. As part of my duties, once other tasks were completed, I would go from bed to bed and chat with the patients. Among the patients was an Army chaplain, a black Baptist preacher who had been a pastor in civilian life. During one conversation with him, I mentioned that I was scheduled to undergo examinations for ordination.

He asked, "Who is preparing you for the examination?"

"No-one," I replied.

"Do you plan to pass the examination?"

"I surely hope so!"

"Only if you are prepared, young man," the chaplain admonished. "Do you know anything about the Eighteen Articles of Faith?"

"What is that?" I asked.

He chuckled and said, "Okay—I will prepare you." He told me how to go about getting all the material I needed, then said, "When you obtain the book with the Eighteen Articles of Faith, commit them to memory."

I did just that.

Ordination and Growth

Day after day, the chaplain drilled me on the questions and answers until he was satisfied that I was prepared.

The council met at Rose of Sharon Baptist Church

in the afternoon of December 29, 1942. I passed the examination with flying colors; according to Pastor White, I scored 95 on the examination and 100 on character.

The ordination service was held that same night. Rev. Charles Smith, pastor of Nazarene Baptist Church preached the ordination sermon. Dr. H. C. Curtis, moderator of the district association, was the catechist.

At the time, the Louisiana Baptist State Convention was holding its winter board meeting at the Rose of Sharon Church. My old friend and mentor Dr. Simon was in attendance; he introduced me to the president of Leland College, who was also present at the conference.

Dr. Bacoats was a well-groomed, nice looking man, and a prince among preachers who encouraged me to come to Leland College School of Religion. Knowing that Dr. Simon had put him up to it, I accepted the invitation and enrolled in the Ministers' course offered to preachers.

To my surprise when I got to Leland, however, Dr. Bacoats was gone. He had agreed to serve as president of Benedict College in South Carolina. He was replaced by a layman in the person of Dr. Frazier, a tall, heavily built man who was a scholar and a good fundraiser and administrator. The dean of the School of Religion was Dr. H. Beecher Hicks Sr. He was a medium-size bald-headed man with a pleasant disposition—a man anyone would like to have for a father.

A Strange Encounter

Back in Alexandria, I was walking up Lee Street near the park one day when a white man coming toward me in the opposite direction stopped me.

"Aren't you a Baptist preacher?" he asked.

"Why, yes," I replied.

He nodded and introduced himself. "I am Reverend _____, and I'm on the staff of the Louisiana Baptist College just across the river in Pineville. Would you do me the honor of coming to our college to meet the president and other faculty members?"

I had no idea what his purpose was. Nonetheless, I accepted his invitation.

I was received very cordially; apparently they had already checked my credentials and character. I was told that the school had an Evangelistic Street Service Program, and they asked me if I would accept their training and orientation in order to participate with them in their outreach street service program.

I accepted their offer. They then asked me to pick out at least three areas in the colored community that would be most conducive for street service.

The college owned a medium-sized bus that had a loudspeaker attached to a full sound system. The bus carried a group of singers from the school and teachers and members of the faculty. I was the only person of color involved. They did the scripture reading, the singing, the praying, and the handing out of flyers; I did the preaching. It was indeed a unique experience.

I learned a lot about saving souls from that group.

Later on, through my efforts, LBC sponsored a class for preachers and laypersons interested in Bible study. The class was held at Nazarene Baptist Church, which was pastored by Reverend Charles Smith. One of students was a Reverend Bob Tyson from Shreveport LA, who became a very close friend. He would frequently visit our worship service at Rose of Sharon.

Black Accomplishments

They're something you rarely hear about. The media today is controlled by Whites. Because of this, the media does not report on issues or accomplishments of Black Americans, instead choosing to focus on the latest scandals of some celebrity. Today, we have an African-American, raised in poverty by a single mother, now on the verge of becoming the first black president of these United States—and what does the media tell us? If they mention him at all, it's about what his wife is wearing, or that he went to the gym! More often, they skip them altogether to report on the daughter of a wealthy white business owner making a scene in a bar. If a black person is involved in a crime or scandal somewhere, all is the better!

It's nothing new. Even back during the war, the media was more interested in anything negative they could report about blacks than focusing on their contributions to the war effort.

As you may know, there were several military bases located around Alexandria. Soldiers stationed in the area would often come to Rose of Sharon to worship. One particular Sunday, a black soldier entered wearing the uniform of an officer in the Army Air Corps. The colleague seated next to me saw the wings the soldier wore on his chest and just about fell out of his seat.

"I didn't know there were colored pilots in the Army!" he whispered to me.

"You never heard of the Tuskegee Airmen?"

It was truly an honor to have that airman in the congregation that Sunday morning. Those black fliers who trained over in Tuskegee, Alabama—many of whom were stationed in Louisiana now for advanced training—were making history. It's a shame more people don't know about their contributions and accomplishments, though.

Winds of Temptation

Although I was a man of the cloth in the service of the Lord, I was also a man of flesh and blood—with all the temptations that come with it. It was all the more difficult for me, as I was still a young man in those days, the juices of life surging through me—and the Lord had seen fit to bless me (or test me, depending on your perspective) by making me most fair for the ladies to look upon.

And I had always had an eye for a nice-looking girl...

My first serious courtship was with a girl I'll call Jane*. She was the daughter of a preacher and loved to sing and play the piano. We met when she came to

---

* Several names in this account have been changed in order to protect the privacy of people involved.

Rose of Sharon, and before I knew what was happening, we were engaged to be married! (This is what you call a "whirlwind courtship.")

Well, one night my cousin Dorothy—who loved dancing—went to a USO dance and saw my fiancée there dancing with a soldier. This was duly reported to me, with no small amount of satisfaction on my cousin's part.

I called Jane and asked her if the story was true. To her credit, she didn't deny it. I told her I'd be over later to discuss the matter.

I was a little torn that night as I walked over to her apartment. I prayed: "Lord, if Jane is not the one You would have me marry, let her return the engagement ring to me without my asking. If she is, let her keep it."

When I arrived, she invited me in, and we sat together on the sofa. I noticed she was not wearing my ring.

When I started to discuss the issue with her, she excused herself, got up and went into her bedroom, and returned a moment later to slip the ring into my hand.

The Lord had given me His answer. That was my cue to leave, and our "whirlwind courtship" ended then and there. However, there was no bitterness, and we remained friends for many years.

Over the years I courted a fair number of young women, but none seriously. I did not feel ready for the commitment of marriage, and this was a source of disappointment and frustration to some of those girls. One in particular was always bringing up the subject of marriage.

The last time I met Marie*, I was seeing her off at the train station as she was leaving for her junior year at college. She brought up the subject of marriage again.

"In due time," I assured her.

She gave me a sad look. "Sam Joubert, by the time you're ready, I'll be pushin' up lilies!"

Then there was Mildred—a young lady whose mother owned and operated a pharmacy and luncheonette on Lee Street.

Mildred had class and beauty, and the attraction between us was almost palpable. We dated a number of times, until one day when I was sitting at her mother's lunch counter chatting with her.

One of the girls from the Rose of Sharon Church (whose name was also Mildred) walked in with a girlfriend of hers. She came up to me and said, "Reverend Joubert, I'd like you to meet Marcia."

When I turned and looked into Marcia's eyes, I was smitten. She had eyes like the Queen of Sheba and a smile like Dorothy Dandridge... everything about her overwhelmed me.

Needless to say, it wasn't long before I was going out with Marcia rather than Mildred. To my recollection, there was hardly a time that I visited her without bringing a gift.

Her father was a dentist and a very active civic worker in our community. I had known her family before; the family was originally from New Orleans, but they relocated to Alexandria when the war broke

---

* Not her real name.

out because the army bases and servicemen's families would provide many new clients.

Marcia was from a family of staunch Catholics. Nevertheless, Marcia would visit our church frequently, which drew me closer to her. I had high hopes that in due time we would get married and she would be the first lady in the church for which I would one day be pastor.

Then came the day that my hopes for matrimonial union with Marcia were shattered.

We were seated on the porch swing together, eating ice cream and talking about the future, when Marcia said, "You know Sam, when we get married, it will be in the Catholic Church, and our children will have to be brought up in the Catholic faith."

I was shocked beyond words. Surely my darling girl knew I was a Baptist preacher, rooted and grounded in the Baptist Church!

My taste for ice cream disappeared. I made an excuse and left her family's home in order to ponder and pray over this unexpected development.

Marcia left for college in North Carolina a few days afterward. After several weeks of prayer and reflection, I sadly took my pen in hand and wrote her the following letter:

January 16th, 1945
Alexandria, LA

Dear Marcia:

With just consideration for you and in answer to

the many nice letters I have received from you, I send this letter as a token of my admiration for your friendship.

But, Marcia, even with our admiration for those we hold as among our dearest friends, we also have convictions, and among those convictions are principles that we must humbly adhere to.

And as we get older and see the light in knowledge of our own grace, we became more set in our ways and convictions to such an extent that we uphold our principles and they become our thoughts, our habits, even our very virtues.

I do not say that every way I go or do is the right way or path, but it will always be the best I know. Now I really believe you feel the same way in your conviction, so it is with sound judgment that unless one of us is fickle in our beliefs (which I now know is not the fact), we would be divided in the things we should cherish the most. And that is in our freedoms of religious beliefs and practice.

Marcia, it doesn't make me think less of you, nor your attitude for your and my differences. It just makes me realize that our paths to the Divine are different, and each of us must travel the path we feel is right.

In closing, Marcia, I have a heartfelt sympathy for you. Knowing each of us, I regret that I must say good-bye.

Sincerely,
Samuel

I am pleased to say that ending our engagement

did not end our friendship, however. She returned that summer, and we continued to see each other on social occasions.

The Serviceman's Family

That summer of 1945, I made the acquaintance of a black soldier who had been a professional band singer in civilian life. The USO was sponsoring a program at which he was to perform, and I was asked to give an address on the theme of "The Serviceman's Family."

The program we rehearsed included this young soldier performing several musical numbers with Dr. LeBeau serving as master of ceremonies. My address was to be delivered between musical numbers.

Today, our US soldiers are being committed to actions all over the world, just as they were over sixty years ago. Whether you consider today's conflicts to be "war," "occupation," or "police action/peacekeeping," the issues faced by our servicemen are basically the same as they were then. I gave this address in 1945, but I feel it is just as timely now as it was in those days. For that reason, my address is included in the appendix at the end of this book.

Chapter VI
A Time of Change

I had made a comfortable life for myself in Alexandria. However, God has a way of shaking and breaking up comfortable complacency—especially when there is new horizon and greater work for one to do in the service of the Lord. Sometimes we can get too comfortable and complacent, so satisfied with our situation that we fail to hear or heed the call to new horizons.

That had become my situation. I was soon to learn that God has a way of shaking your very foundation, which in some instances means giving up your comfortable home environment in order to go to some far-off place among complete strangers where God has a greater assignment for you.

More Responsibility

Some time after my ordination, I purchased my first automobile—a 1942 Chevrolet four-door sedan. The purchase of a motor vehicle proved to be fortuitous.

Shortly after I bought the car, Pastor White took ill, and his responsibilities and duties fell to me. The car came in handy; after my first time serving Holy Communion as pastor, I took the chairman of the deacons and the chairperson of the deaconesses ministry and served Communion to the pastor in Bunkie, which is about twelve miles from Alexandria. Having a vehicle made the trip much easier and faster.

After Pastor White's recovery, I traveled with him to his other church about twenty miles away, the Little Rock Baptist Church near Morrow.

I preached and helped him serve Communion. When I got through preaching, the chairman of the deacons remarked to me, "You know, Reverend Joubert... when Pastor White introduced you as the guest preacher for today, I wondered why he had brought a mere boy to preach to us."

He grinned at me and put a hand on my shoulder, then added, "After hearing you preach, I take it all back." He turned to Pastor White and said, "Samuel may look like a boy, but he preaches like a man!"

A few Sundays later, Pastor White turned to me during the service and said, "Please stand, Reverend Joubert. I have a special announcement to make about you."

He then turned to the congregation and said, "I took my son in the ministry to my church in Morrow, and the people fell in love with him." He then expressed his wish to make me the assistant pastor.

The flock shouted "AMEN!" Pastor White turned to me and grinned. "Now don't you get in too big a hurry, son—you won't get this post until I die!"

Adjustments

The house that I shared with my grandmother, Aunt Virginia, and sister Clara had two bedrooms. The three women slept in one, and I in the other. This happy arrangement was not to last, however.

My sister Clara was a looker—five-foot-nine, long black hair, and dark eyes. She was always a snappy dresser, and men rarely failed to notice her. At one point, Clara had two suitors between whom she was trying to decide. One of the men looked to be a *mulatto* and was quite worldly. The other was darker, taller, and loved to talk about church and spiritual matters.

Realizing it was Clara's choice, I nonetheless expressed my liking for the latter and his spiritual-mindedness—but said no more on the matter.

In due time, I noticed that Clara was seeing the church-minded young man exclusively. After his draft number came up, she received letters from him nearly every week. Then, when he came home on furlough, they were married.

Before long, my new brother-in-law—whose name was Freddie Alexander—received a medical discharge and came home for good. Clara and her new husband took over my bedroom, and I wound up sleeping on the living room sofa, which folded out into a bed.

Many Are Called...

My preaching ministry at this time was in full bloom. Having a car enabled me to accept when I was called on to preach in many of the Baptist Churches in our region of the state as well as the district association. I recall conducting a revival at the Baptist Church in Pineville. Reverend H. Y. Wood, who served on my ordination committee, had me preaching regularly at both of his churches, one of which was located several miles away in Bunkie. When Pastor White became too ill, I found myself again in charge of both Rose of Sharon and Little Rock in Morrow.

One Sunday evening, I arrived at the Rose of Sharon Church for services and was greeted by Sister Louise Hood, the missionary president and perhaps the one most powerful member of the church.

"Reverend," she said, "I have a little surprise for you." She turned and presented a handsome, well-groomed young man. "Willie White is here, and he says he is called to preach."

I nodded. Willie was Pastor White's youngest son—a highly educated college graduate who ran a funeral home up in Bunkie. I shook Willie's hand and greeted him. "Brother Willie, you go get ready to preach, and I will call on you when preaching time arrives."

We started the evening worship serve as usual, but when preaching hour came, I announced that I would not be delivering the sermon. "I will lead you in song," I announced, "and afterward, our pastor's son Willie will bring you the message for tonight."

Willie White delivered his initial sermon. It was well delivered and well prepared.

A few weeks later Pastor White was well enough to come back to the pulpit and resume his duties as pastor. He thanked me for what I did for his son, saying, "You did what I would not have done. You allowed him to preach his first sermon in the pulpit, whereas I would have had him preach on the floor in front of the pulpit. However," he added, "I suppose the

Lord wanted it done the way it was done."

Meanwhile, Reverend H. Y. Wood passed on, and I was the leading candidate to take his place. However, when the deacons met to call a pastor, my name had been dropped, and they called upon a colleague of mine who was better known as a musician than a preacher. I was troubled by this, because I knew the church officers there and I had been assured that I was the congregation's choice.

Ten years later, I learned why I had been called but not chosen. The pulpit committee had met with Pastor White. One of them had said, "We want you to know that we want Reverend Joubert to be our next pastor."

Pastor White had said to them, "I need him by my side… you cannot have him." That ended it. It was an honor, but strangely, Pastor White never informed me about this decision.

End of the Beginning

Up to this point, my life in Alexandria—going to school, learning, working, growing, and socializing—had been an experience of joy and comfort, despite moments of anxiety. All of that was soon to come to an end.

It had started with my sister's marriage and subsequent disruption of my home life. Then my hopes of filling the vacancy left by Reverend Wood's passing were dashed (I did not then know Pastor White's role in this or his reasoning). A few months later the same thing happened with another vacant church a few miles outside of Alexandria where a number of my schoolmates were members and had assured me I was the leading candidate for the post.

There was also the issue of Marcia, who was back in Alexandria for the summer. Although I had ended our engagement, Marcia was very strong-willed and determined to have her own way with me. I had begun to weaken—not that I would agree to all she suggested. I nonetheless saw myself bending a little to the extent that I might compromise myself under her strong, feminine influence. My better judgment kept saying, "Bertie, you need to get away from this situation."

A still, small voice within me kept calling upon me to go to New York City, of all places! I didn't understand. Why not back home to Opelousas? Why not Washington, Shreveport, or Lake Charles? If I must go to a big city, why not New Orleans? If I must leave my beloved Louisiana, why not Port Arthur, Texas—which was not all that far away, and where I had least had an uncle?

As I pondered over the matter, something happened that convinced me that the time had come for me to pack up and move on to where God was leading me.

I was in attendance at one of the Baptist District Association quarterly sessions. When we recessed for lunch, an old, one-armed preacher who was well liked and respected by all called me aside to give me a word of advice.

"Young man," he said, "I have watched you for some time. You have a good reputation and a promising bright future. There is only one problem; you are in a precarious situation."

"Go on," I said.

He continued, "You are well liked by the parishioners at Rose of Sharon Baptist Church. If Pastor White died today, you would be called to be the next pastor because you are first in the hearts of the members. However," he said, "the problem you face is the fact that the son of Pastor White is now preaching.

"You are the Pastor's son in the ministry, but Willie is his blood son. You are the only one standing between the Pastor, his son, and the church." He finished by saying, "This is not a situation you want to be in. You are young, gifted, and promising young preacher, and your field is the world. God has a place for you — get out of that one as soon as possible."

Well! I'd been pondering over leaving, and this shocking revelation forced me to give definite, serious thought and to pray for guidance and direction from my Heavenly Father. His answer was not long in coming.

It was a hot summer day when I went to Hospital Ward #194 at Camp Claiborne and tendered my resignation to the sergeant on duty. He couldn't believe it. "Where are you going?" he asked.

"New York City," I replied.

The next day, I drove down to Grand Prairie in order to get my parents' blessing. At first, Mama cried, "Son, I can't see you going all the way to New York. Why so far?"

"That is where the Lord is leading me," I replied softly.

"There you go again, telling me what the Lord is saying to you!" she said. Then she sighed and put her hand on my cheek. "You know I would not dare interfere with what the Lord is telling you to do."

Reluctantly, sadly, Mama and Papa gave me their blessing to leave for New York City. I spent the night there in my old room and returned to Alexandria the next day. As I drove up US 90 toward what would not be home much longer, I wondered how I would go about telling the flock at Rose of Sharon that I would be leaving them. My moving away with no plans to return at this point might cause confusion; they might even pressure Pastor White to name me his successor just to keep me from leaving. Remembering what had been told me at the BDA session, though, my mind was made up—I had to go.

I told Pastor White and the Rose of Sharon congregation that I was going to New York City to further my studies in the ministry for the next nine months—which was true. What I did not tell them was I had no plans of returning afterwards.

I was given a going away party second to none. The gathering was at the home of the chairman of the deacon board. He was a starkly built tall man, light brown in color with long, strong arms and large hands, a big-hearted Christian who most of the time had a broad smile and a glad handshake for everybody. I was loaded down with gifts, which lasted for years. My family, friends, and parishioners all prayed and cried over me as I left the party.

The next day I went to the store and bought a trunk, a large luggage bag, and a medium-size luggage bag. I packed all I could and bid good-bye to my grandmother Elmira and my aunt Virginia. I had my friend and co-worker Kirkland, to whom I had sold my car, drive Freddie, Clara, and myself to the railroad station, where I purchased my ticket. I checked all the luggage and had them placed in the baggage car. I took a final look at my surroundings and shook hands with Kirkland, shook hands with my brother-in-law Fred, and kissed my sister Clara goodbye one last time before boarding the train with a prayer on my lips. As the trained pulled out of the station, I waved a last goodbye to everyone.

I saw Clara beating back the tears from her eyes.

As the lush forests and swamplands of Louisiana passed by, I realized that another chapter in my life had come to a close. I was on the verge of the beginning of a new chapter in my life. I was like Abraham hearing, listening, and obeying the voice of He who said, "I Am that I Am; the Alpha and Omega, the First and the Last, the Beginning and the Ending."

Chapter VII
Far from Home

…I have been a stranger in a strange land.
—Exodus 2:22.

Moses' reflections upon naming his firstborn in a land far from home were in my mind as my train was fast approaching Grand Central Station and the City of New York. I was going to a place where I would indeed be like Moses, a "stranger in a strange land." I had made no arrangements as to where I would spend the first night on my arrival. I was totally leaning and depending on God for whatever the future had to offer.

As the train pulled into the station, I found reassurance in the words of David, who, when surrounded by the pagan Philistines, wrote in Psalm 121:

> *I will lift up my eyes to the hills, From whence cometh my help? My help cometh from the LORD, the maker of heaven and earth. He will not let your foot slip. He who watches over you will not slumber…*

That scripture was the pillar and ground upon which my whole future was to be built and sustained. I was prepared to begin the new chapter in my life.

Day One

I got off the train sometime after 10 a.m. on the morning of August 15, 1945. Grand Central Station was a big place and utterly strange to me. I went directly to the travelers aid desk and spoke to a middle-age white lady who was very cordial and helpful.

I told her who I was and that I needed a nice place to stay. "The first thing you should do is rent one of those lockers over there," she said, pointing toward that part of the station, "and store your luggage. They'll give you a key. Then you go over to Forty-second Street, keep walking until you see the YMCA, and they'll rent you a room."

I did exactly as she instructed me and found the place. I went in and inquired for a room of the white man at the desk with a large ledger. There was a tall, white gentleman right behind me and several others behind him.

He looked up at me, started to turn pages in a very disinterested fashion, and said, "I'm sorry, we have no vacancies."

I turned and slowly walked away dejected. As I reached the sidewalk in front of the YMCA building, I stood still for a brief moment to think of what my next move would be. To my surprise that same tall, white man who had been standing behind me came out of the building and over to me. He said, "I'm from Canada—like you, I just arrived. I have to tell you, that the chap at the desk in there was lying to you. I was right behind you, and he gave me a room."

This revelation shook me up and made me look for

a black person to talk to. I finally saw a young black boy and told him what had happened.

He looked me over and said, "Mister, you's lookin' for a room in the wrong part o' town. You need to go to Harlem."

"Is there a YMCA in Harlem?"

"Over on 135th."

"How do I get there?"

The boy took me to the subway and showed me where to buy tokens, which train to get on, and where to get off.

I can never forget my first ride on the subway, under the ground. I could hardly believe my eyes.

I got off at 135th Street and found the Harlem YMCA, just as the boy had told me. I went in and found a very nice-looking black woman at the desk. When I inquired about a room, however, she replied in a very odd dialect that I could not understand. I asked her to repeat what she had said, but her speech was incomprehensible to me, so I left.

I wound up finding a nearby hotel where I rented a room for two nights. I paid six dollars in advance, took my room key and receipt, and walked out, intending to fetch my luggage from the station.

I asked directions from the first man I saw on the street. No doubt noting my Southern accent, he said, "You're new here, aren't you?"

I nodded. "I am the Reverend Samuel Joubert from Alexandria, Louisiana," I said, offering him my hand.

He nodded. "I *thought* you were someone special. I watched you going in and comin' out. Now, lemme give you some advice.

"Don' ask directions from *anyone* you see on the street. This here's NYC—somebody's liable to lead you into an alleyway, knock you in the head, and steal you blind—or worse. You need directions, you find a cop."

Next, the man indicated the hotel from which I had just emerged. "Next thing—you don' wanna stay in that hotel. That there's a clip joint—ain't no place for a young minister. Go back and ask for your money back. He prob'ly won't give it all, but tell 'im you changed your mind and you'll split the difference with 'im. That's what I did."

Noting my look of dismay, he grinned. "Look, man—I jes' got here from Connecticut. What say we look for a place together?"

My new friend's name was Jeff Robinson. We finally found adjoining rooms at the Hudson Hotel on Amsterdam Avenue near 143rd Street, which is where I spent my first night in New York City.

The next morning, Jeff knocked on my door.

"Jeff—good morning!"

"Man, we can't stay here—I woke up in the middle of the night and saw bed-bugs crawlin' 'round my room—you prob'ly got 'em too."

No, that would never do. Next to Godliness, cleanliness has always been my priority. When we checked out, we met the doorman and asked him if he knew where we would find a Baptist preacher with whom I could speak.

"Reverend Doctor George Sims," he said. "He's in the phone book."

The NYC phone book was as large then as it is today, but we managed to locate his number and gave him a call.

Dr. Sims agreed to see us. His home was located on 133rd Street between Lenox and Seventh Avenue. His son, Reverend George Sims Jr., met us at the door and led us through their well-appointed flat to his father's study.

Dr. Sims was a tall and prominent-looking man with a withered left hand. I removed my hat respectfully and introduced myself and my companion. I said, "I have come to New York to further my study in the ministry, and I need a place to stay along with this gentleman."

Dr. Sims picked up the receiver of the phone on his desk and asked the operator for a number. After a moment, he said in an authoritative voice, "Good morning, this is Brother Sims speaking. I have two gentlemen here. One is a preacher who looks like he's somebody, and his companion. I am sending them over. Please arrange some lodging for them."

Dr. Sims then turned to Jeff and me. "Go on back to the YMCA on 135th," he said. "They will take care of you."

We returned to the YMCA to find the same girl who had been on duty the day before. This time, however, she came out from behind the desk and pointed me toward the building across the street, which was called the Annex.

It was there that I was able to secure lodgings at a cost of six dollars per week. Jeff, who did not care to stay at the YMCA, found a room in a private home up the street.

I had arrived in NYC with a little over $151 in my

pocket. In those days, bus and subway fare was a nickel, and you could eat very well for two or more dollars.

Tempted Again

The Lord seems to give all of us some cross to bear—a weakness on which we are tested again and again. Mine, as you know, was a pretty girl.

My first encounter with a young woman in NY taught me a lesson I would always remember. Near the Hudson Hotel on Amsterdam Avenue around the Washington Heights area, I found a restaurant and had a nice meal. The waitress who served me was a black girl, a few years my senior. I ate there on a number of times, and she invited me to visit her. She was nice looking with a nice figure, and she knew how to entice a young man green as grass.

Now, while working at the hospital at Camp Claiborne, LA, I saw many of our young soldiers who had been enticed by women, with the result that some of them had syphilis, gonorrhea, and other such venereal diseases transmitted through sexual contact. What I saw would turn your stomach inside out.

With that in mind, I asked her if she had ever been infected by any of those diseases. In the twinkling of an eye that young woman changed from a charming, affectionate female to a cobra.

She turned on me with fire in her eyes and said, "If you don't get out of here as fast as you can, I will NOT be responsible for what happens to you!"

I did just that: out I went. As I reflected on that

incident, I came to the conclusion that she was perhaps at the time or some previous time affected by some such female disease. If not, she was a hellcat of a woman that I'd be better off without. The good Lord was watching out for me that day.

Exploring My New Home

My friend Jeff turned out to be a guiding light indeed. He was an older man who had been to New York previously.

One day, he advised me, "Reverend, I am certain you will one day be a great pastor in this city. Problem is, you're young, and no-one knows you around here.

"Now's a good time for you to become acquainted with the kind of life your people are living so you will know what and how to preach to them."

Over the next two weeks, I allowed myself a bit of a vacation while Jeff took me on a tour of Harlem and all the "hot spots": the Savoy Ballroom, the Big Apple, the Apollo Theatre and others—not to take part, but simply to observe what was going on.

By the end of that two weeks, I realized my money would not last forever. It was time to look for a job. Because of my civil service experience, it was fairly easy for me to secure a position with the US Post Office.

Now that I had a steady source of income, my next task was to find a spiritual home. There was an elderly man at the YMCA who was very friendly and loved to chew the fat. I asked him if there was a Baptist Church in Harlem he could recommend.

"Son," he said, "there is only one church in Harlem I recommend going to, and that is the Abyssinian Baptist Church, which is my home church." After a few visits to the Abyssinian Church, I did join the congregation there.

Dr. Adam Clayton Powell Sr., was the pastor emeritus. His son, Adam Clayton Powell Jr., was the pastor, but had also recently been elected to the US House of Representatives—the first African-American congressman from any northern state in more than seventy years. His constituents in Harlem would continue to send him back to Congress for the next twenty-six years.

The Reverend Powell Jr. was a tall man with a long, sharp nose and features that looked more European than African; unless he told you he was colored, he might easily have passed for white. The associate pastor was man from Barbados in the West Indies named David Nathaniel Licorish. He was a very astute preacher with an overwhelming personality and was a great orator in his own right.

The Abyssinian Baptist Church was, and still is, one of NYC's great historical, spiritual, and even musical institutions. At the time I was there, it was one of the largest Protestant congregations in the USA. The father of jazz piano, the great Thomas "Fats" Waller, was once a minister there; during the previous decade, the great German pastor Dietrich Bonhoeffer, who fled to the US when Hitler came to power, would attend the ABC on occasion. The legendary entertainer Nat King Cole would marry his second wife at Abyssinian less than three years later. During the "Harlem

Renaissance," Abyssinian was the center of sacred music as much as the nearby Cotton Club was for secular jazz; you'll still hear the finest gospel singing anywhere at the Abyssinian Baptist Church.

About My Father's Business

I decided it was time to get on with the purpose for which the Lord had sent me to New York. I enrolled in the Bible Institute over on Fifty-fifth Street, taking evening classes and working at a post office near Sixty-third Street during the day.

At the time I was hired, I informed the supervisor that I would not work on the Sabbath Day, nor evenings, which I needed free for classes at the Institute. Nonetheless, after several months as a postal worker, I noticed a change in my working schedule posted on the board from days to evenings—including Sundays.

I spoke to the lady in the office about it. She said, "There is nothing we can do here at this station, but you should go back to Thirty-third Street where you were hired, and they may make adjustments."

Just in case, I started looking for a new job in my spare time. I wound up taking a position as an orderly at Harlem Hospital, shortly before I resigned from the post office. The job at Harlem Hospital was days, Monday through Friday with weekends off.

More Temptation—and Demon Rum

During my stay at the YMCA Annex, I met a soldier who was a captain and had done some undercover work in the service. Whenever he was in the New York area he would stay at the Harlem YMCA. We became acquaintances, and one night he asked me to accompany him to visit his lady friend.

We went to a place on 145th Street, where I met his lady friend and another young girl who was apparently rooming with her. The young lady with me in the living room was eighteen years old; her name was Edna, and she was a charming young lady with a broad smile and enchanting eyes.

It wasn't long before the captain and his lady friend left us in the living room and took refuge in the bedroom.

We talked some, then "petted" for a while, but she made it clear that if I had anything else in mind that I should forget it. Later, when that captain and I left, she invited me to call on her again. However, when I attempted to find her again she had moved.

I had just about forgotten about Edna when I received a call from her saying she wanted to see me again. I visited her in her new location on 147th Street near Broadway.

We became close friends. Edna believed in giving nice gifts and showered me with them. She worked as a governess for rich folks who lived on Fifty-ninth Street overlooking Central Park. She talked so much about me to her employer that they finally allowed her to have me visit her one day while she was at work.

I can never forget that visit. It was the first time I got on an elevator that opened into someone's private in apartment. I met her employer, who greeted me cordially. After a while she and the lady of the house asked me what would I like to drink. They named all manner of strong drinks, but I would drink ginger ale only. They repaired to the kitchen and came back with a large, deep glass full of what I thought was ginger ale.

I drank it up and not long afterward was in rapid conversation. Whenever I would attempt to drive home a point I had a habit of standing up. However, when I stood up this time, my head felt like it was my feet—and I knew then that the drink served me was something stronger than ginger ale. I immediately found an excuse to leave.

All I can remember was getting off the elevator and walking toward the subway. From then on I remember nothing until I woke up the next morning in my bed at the YMCA, my head pounding. I don't recall getting on the subway nor getting off, neither do I recall walking from the subway to the YMCA, taking my clothes off, and going to bed.

The only thing I can say is that the Lord must have had an angel to guide me all the way to my bed. Whatever they had given me had made me drunk as a skunk.

Later I called Edna and gave her a good tongue-lashing. Edna confessed they'd mixed Scotch whiskey and several other strong drinks into my ginger ale. She said they wanted to play a joke on me all in fun, but to me this was no fun.

Family Reunion

My cousin Lincoln had recently been mustered out

of the Army and had returned home to find me gone. Having been informed by my mother of my whereabouts, he immediately wrote me a letter indicating his desire to join me in NYC if I could arrange suitable lodgings.

Would I?

Straight away I spoke to the manager at the YMCA, who assured me that my cousin would have a room upon his arrival.

Not only Lincoln, but my other cousin Matthew showed up a few days later. It was a truly joyous reunion, as the three of us had been more like brothers than cousins.

In the meantime, I tried to make an appointment with the younger Dr. Powell for discussing how he might assist me in fulfilling my desire to minister to the people of Harlem. Now, all the officers and members of the Abyssinian Baptist Church were always very kind to me, but Dr. Powell, being a US Congressman as well as a pastor, was simply too busy to see me.

Having served in the role of acting pastor in Louisiana, I knew that unless I got to the pastor of the church and secured his blessings, the hands of the congregation would be tied in helping me to move forward, no matter how much they cared. I therefore started to look for another church home. After visiting a number of churches in Harlem, I found the Mt. Olivet Baptist Church, located at the corner of 120th Street and Lenox Avenue, where I was greatly inspired by the preaching of Dr. O. Clay Maxwell Sr. and his son O. Clay Maxwell Jr.

I sought membership there and was accepted. The

following summer, I was retained as one of the teachers for the vacation church school for two or three weeks with a stipend of fifty dollars—a great deal of money in those days. For recreation, we took the children to Central Park, the Bronx Zoo, and boating on the nearby Indian Pond. It was a great and pleasant experience for me.

Doris

While in New York, I had written a number of letters to Rose of Sharon, expressing my thanks and appreciation for their kindness to me. I also received a letter from Pastor White. However, it was not even two years after leaving Alexandria that I received word reporting that Pastor White had gone to be with the Lord. Not long after his passing, his son Willie White was called to pastor the Rose of Sharon Church.

I'd had a taste of broadcasting before leaving Louisiana, and the drive to get on the air was like a fever I could not shake. In 1946, I began to make inquiries as to whom I could talk with or who could help me in this matter. I was told to go to the Salvation Army Center and ask for a lady named Etta Stroud.

I went there and met the lady. Etta said, "I'll see what I can do to help you… but in the meantime, I have something I would like for you to do for me."

"Of course," I replied.

She said, "Every Saturday afternoon we have Bible Study in the Chapel of the center. Will you come and be our teacher?"

I consented. It proved to be one of the great turning

points of my life.

The following Saturday I took my cousin Matthew Stephens with me and taught the Bible class in the chapel on the second floor. I noticed a charming young lady among others in the class who kept writing most of the time. When the class ended, she disappeared.

Later as Sister Stroud, Matthew, and I were walking down the stairs to the first floor, this same young lady was coming up the steps. Mrs. Stroud stopped her and said, "Doris, I want you to meet these fine young men."

"Oh Mrs. Stroud, I'm sick of meeting men," she complained wearily.

I said, "What do you want to meet, women?" When she took a second look and saw that one of the men was the teacher of the Bible class, her countenance became almost apologetic.

Ms. Doris Joyce Lee Thorpe. She was as pretty as a young filly and just as innocent and unbridled. I had just met the young lady who was destined to become my life's companion in marriage.

Photographs

Rev. Dr. Samuel B. Joubert, Sr.

Florestine Ardoin Joubert,
paternal grandmother of
Rev. Dr. Samuel B. Joubert, Sr.

Elmira Robert Wickliffe,
maternal grandmother of
Dr. Samuel B. Joubert, Sr.

Edmond & Virgie Joubert & Son Eldridge

Virgie Wickliffe Joubert, mother of Rev. Dr. Samuel B. Joubert, Sr.

Edna Athay, second fiancée of Rev. Dr. Samuel B. Joubert, Sr.

Dr. Grover Cleveland Williams. He married Rev. Dr. & Mrs. Samuel B. Joubert, Sr.

Rev. Dr. Samuel B. Joubert, Sr., 1947

Rev. Dr. Samuel B. Joubert, Sr.

Rev. Dr. Samuel B. Joubert, Sr. performing wedding ceremony at Community Baptist Church, Bayside, NY

Borough President Ed Dudley, Dr. Joseph H. Jackson, President National Baptist Convention, USA, Inc. and Rev. Dr. Samuel B. Joubert, Sr.

Rev. Dr. Samuel B. Joubert, Sr. & his wife Rev. Doris Joubert

Rev. Dr. Samuel B. Joubert, Sr. & his son in the Ministry, Dr. Richard Wills, Pastor, First Baptist Church, Hampton, Virginia

The Joubert Family

Standing L-R: Phyllis McKoy Joubert, Rev. Dr. Samuel B. Joubert, Sr., Renay Joubert, Gala Derene Joubert

Seated L-R: Rev. Samuel B. Joubert, Jr., David Eugene Joubert, Deborah Joubert McCampbell, Joseph Edward Joubert, Rev. Dr. Phillip Charles Joubert, Sr.

Rev. Dr. Samuel B. Joubert, Sr. conducting worship service on the boat in the Sea of Galilee in Israel, 1993

Rev. Dr. Samuel B. Joubert, Sr. conducting worship service in the Upper Room in Jerusalem, 1993

Rev. Dr. Samuel B. Joubert, Sr. at special conference, shaking hands with NYC Mayor Robert Wagner & Borough President Ed Dudley in the center.

Rev. Dr. Samuel B. Joubert, Sr., Dr. T. J. Jemison, President, National Baptist Convention, USA, Inc., and Rev. Doris Joubert

Dr. William J. Harvey, III, Executive Secretary, Foreign Mission Board, Rev. Dr. Samuel B. Joubert, Sr., 1987

Rev. Dr. Samuel B. Joubert, Sr. leaving the tomb of Jesus Christ in Jerusalem, 1993

L-R: Rev. Dr. Samuel B. Joubert, Sr., Dr. Franklyn Richardson, Pastor, Grace B.C., Mt. Vernon, NY, Chairman of the Board of the National Action Committee, Dr. John Kenney, Dean of School of Religion, Virginia Union, Richmond, Virginia

Rev. Dr. Samuel B. Joubert, Sr., presenting vacation purse to Dr. Allen Paul Weaver, President, Baptist Ministers' Conference of Greater NY & Vicinity, 1993

Dr. William Leo Hamilton, Pastor, Bethany B.C., Jamaica, NY, President of Baptist Ministers' Conference, Rev. Floyd Flake, Civic Day preacher/speaker, Rev. Dr. Samuel B. Joubert, Sr., Chairman, Civic Committee

President Lyons, Rev. Al Sharpton, Rev. Dr. Samuel B. Joubert, Sr. at Reception for President Lyons at Canaan, B.C., NYC

L-R: Missionary (to Africa) Josephine Minter, Rev. Dr. Samuel B. Joubert, Sr., Dr. Thomas J. Boyd, Former Pastor, Salem Missionary B.C., Brooklyn, NY (over 40 years), Strongest Mission Supporter

Rev. Dr. Samuel B. Joubert, Sr., Rev. Charles Kenyatta, former bodyguard of Malcolm X, now deceased.

Dr. Richard Wills, Pastor, First Baptist Church, Hampton, Virginia, Rev. Doris Joubert, Rev. Dr. Samuel B. Joubert, Sr., Deacon Cooper & wife Charity

Dr. David Nathaniel Licorish, Assistant to Rev. Adam Clayton Powell, Abyssinian, B.C., NYC, Rev. Dr. Samuel B. Joubert, Sr.

Dr. H. DeVore Chapman, Pastor, Greater Bright Light B.C. Brooklyn, NY, Pastor, Bethel B.C., Brooklyn, NY, Recording Secretary, Board of Directors, National Baptist Convention, USA, Inc., Rev. Dr. Samuel B. Joubert, Sr.

Rev. Dr. Samuel B. Jordan, Pastor of Gethsemane, B.C., Philadelphia, PA. His church is the highest contributor in the National Baptist Convention, Inc. giving $50,000.00 annually to foreign missions, Rev. Dr. Samuel B. Joubert, Sr., Recording Secretary of the Foreign Mission Board.

Mrs. Gloria Jones, Vice President, Women's Auxiliary, the National Baptist Convention, USA, Inc. & Rev. Dr. Samuel B. Joubert, Sr.

Sister Geraldine Gilchrist & Rev. Doris Joubert

Rev. Doris Joubert & Sister Geraldine Gilchrist

L-R: Dr. Calvin E. Owens, First VP, Baptist Ministers' Conference, Dr. James Wilson, Jr., President, Baptist Ministers' Conference, Rev. Dr. Samuel B. Joubert, Sr., Senior Living Former President, BMC, Rev. Dr. Phillip Charles Joubert, Sr., the only one to succeed his father, Rev. Dr. Samuel B. Joubert, Sr. as President of Conference in 107 years.

The Joubert Family L-R: Rev. Dr. Phillip Charles Joubert, Sr., Deborah Joubert McCampbell, Rev. Samuel B. Joubert, Jr., Rev. Dr. Samuel B. Joubert, Sr., Joseph Edward Joubert, Rev. Doris Thorpe Joubert, David Eugene Joubert, Sr.

L-R: Dr. Joe Albert Bush, Executive Secretary, Foreign Mission Board, National Baptist Convention, USA, Inc., Dr. Naomi Tyler Lloyd, Pastor, Trinity Baptist Church, Foreign Mission Drive Guest Preacher, Rev. Dr. Samuel B. Joubert, Sr., NYS Chairman, Commission on Foreign Missions, Dr. Washington Lundy, President, Empire State Convention

Rev. Dr. Samuel B. Joubert, Sr. Preaching at Baptist Ministers' Conference, Convent Avenue B.C., Former President, President's Day, 2004

Service Award Plaque
From the National Baptist Convention, USA, Inc.
53 Years of Pastoring

CHAPTER VIII
FINDING MY PLACE

Although I had met my future spouse and helpmate, I did not know it at the time—and I had much to experience and learn before that union was destined to happen.

Reverend Salisberry and the Choir

A young man starting out in any career requires two things—a network of like-minded people to assist him and a mentor to guide him. Back in Louisiana, I had been fortunate to have two wonderful mentors, Dr. Simon and Pastor White.

In 1946, I was introduced to the local Baptist Minister's Conference, which met every Monday at the Metropolitan Baptist Church on 128th Street and Seventh Avenue. I also became a member of the Baptist Minister's Conference of Greater New York and Vicinity as well.

It was during my attendance at the conference that I met one Reverend A. M. Salisberry, who had recently come to NYC from Cleveland, Ohio—but like myself, who was originally from Louisiana. Salisberry was a good-looking, dark-skinned man who always dressed in the best of clothing, wore dark-rimmed glasses, and as a preacher, singer, and leader of prayer was nearly in a class to himself. He was what you might call a "smooth talker" or a "shrewd operator"; he could charm the fat right out of a cooked biscuit.

As we were both natives of "The Pelican State," we wound up becoming friends—although, ultimately, I would discover we had little in common beyond that. Such a realization came much later, however; for now, he latched onto me like white on rice.

I introduced him to most of my friends and told him I was a member of Mt. Olivet Baptist Church. He sized up my situation there and said, "You are wasting your time sitting around waiting Sunday after Sunday for a chance to read the scripture or perhaps give the invocation. You can forget about being asked to preach on Sunday morning."

Salisberry reminded me of the fact that Mt. Olivet was well supplied with preaching between Pastor Maxwell and his son. "You and the other local preachers are like extra baggage just hanging around," he said. "In the first place the Lord didn't call you to simply hang around, and secondly you aren't hanging around material."

Then he finally made a useful suggestion: "Get out in the field where you can utilize your talent and grow." His idea was to organize a choir. "Most churches love good singing at various churches," he pointed out. "We will get to be known, the choir will be asked to sing, and we will asked to preach."

This seemed like an excellent idea. I wrote Mama and asked her to suggest a name for the choir. She wrote back and suggested we call it the Shadows of Gethsemane.

That was the name we settled on, and as the Shadows of Gethsemane Gospel Choir grew, the group became greatly in demand among congregations throughout the city. The choir's performances opened doors to opportunities for both of us to sing and preach.

Salisberry predicted, "Through this choir, at least one of us will be called to a church—and there, we will be co-pastors."

That is exactly how it happened. One afternoon, the choir sang at the St. John Baptist Church of West 152nd Street. Salisberry was asked to pray, and in his prayer he mentioned how God had brought him all the way from the clay hills of Louisiana. It so happened that one of the members of the church was also from our home state. She had a sister who was a member of another church that was looking for a pastor.

Eventually, this woman introduced Salisberry to her sister, and he was given a chance to preach at the church. Afterwards, he was called as pastor.

The church was located on 117th Street, between Eighth Avenue and Manhattan Avenue and was known as the Gethsemane Baptist Church.

Despite the fact that Reverend Salisberry assured me that we were "co-pastors," I of course had sense enough to know a church can't have two pastors at the same time. I have learned that no matter what position you have, be it co-pastor, assistant pastor, assistant to the pastor or associate minister, there is only one pastor at a time. The responsibility of leading, instructing, and overseeing the membership and the church proper is the pastor's role; all others are his helpers and are to carry out his instructions and his program as he is instructed by the great head of the church, who is Jesus the Christ.

So, I served at Gethsemane as assistant pastor.

It was about this time that I moved out of my lodgings at the YMCA and took a room with another pastor from Louisiana. Reverend G. C. Williams was, like Salisberry, from Shreveport, and was serving as the pastor of the Cosmopolitan Baptist Church on West 157th Street. Reverend Salisberry told me that Pastor Williams and his wife had a spare room that they wished to let to a Christian man.

He convinced me to go check the room out. The moment I met G. C. Williams and his wife, our spirits blended—and not long afterward I left the Y and moved to the church house living quarters.

Little did I know at the time that Pastor G. C. Williams would be the one to perform my marriage right there in the Cosmopolitan Baptist Church—and that my new bride and I would spend our honeymoon in one of the apartments above the church's sanctuary.

But all of that was still in the future.

Returning Home

It was about this time that I received the sorrowful news that my sister Estella had died. There was no way I would be able to take a train and arrive home in time for the funeral—so I wound up traveling by airplane for the first time.

Now, I'd always felt that if the good Lord had meant man to fly, He would have given him wings like

Finding My Place

a bird—flying was nothing I wanted to do. It was the only way I would be able to attend my sister's funeral, however—so I reluctantly made the arrangements.

While at the airport waiting for the flight that would take me from New Orleans to Alexandria, I became hungry and asked the shoeshine man would they serve me if I went in the airport restaurant.

He said, "Yes, but they will place a screen around you. That is what they do when they serve black people." Not willing to be subject to that sort of inhumane treatment, I chose to go hungry and wait to be served on board the plane.

While I was back home in Louisiana, I had the opportunity to go up to Alexandria, where I had spent so many happy years, and visit the Rose of Sharon Baptist Church. My old mentor, Pastor White, had passed on by this time, and the pulpit had been taken over by his son, Willie.

I was received and treated with love and respect by the new Pastor White and the congregation and was called on to preach. Afterwards, they took up an offering for me. I noticed the members were very generous in their giving; the offering was at least forty or fifty dollars. Therefore, I was a little surprised when they gave me a check for seventeen dollars.

One of the trustees was a lady friend who was very fond of me. I asked her what was the reason for shortchanging me. She said, "We felt that you did not need the money, since you came by plane and you had on the best of clothing and were very liberal in giving in the church offering." Let me say emphatically the pastor was not to blame; the trustees were the ones who made that decision.

I recall Reverend Dr. Williams telling me how he'd had similar experiences. He had preached at a particular church a number of times; when they would take up the offering for the preacher, the officers would grab it from the table and go in the back room to count the offering. Invariably, they would come back with far less than what was taken off the table. He decided to put a stop to these shenanigans.

On this occasion they took up an offering for him as usual. However, as they were about to grab the money off the table he stood on his feet and said: "Brother Pastor, is that offering really for me?"

The Pastor replied, "Why, yes, Reverend."

Reverend Williams then pulled out a large handkerchief from his pocket and said, "Brethren, since that offering is for me, here is my handkerchief—just tie it up and hand it to me, I'll count it at home."

When I heard that story, I laughed and said, "Amen!"

Unfortunately, too much of this is being done even now.

Despite what had happened at Rose of Sharon, I would continue to visit and preach at Rose of Sharon on my return visits to Alexandria.

Temptation—Again

Again and again, the Lord was determined to test my strength of will against my natural urges as a man of flesh.

Finding My Place

It was during my second visit to Alexandria. I was staying at the home of my sister Clara and her husband, Freddy. My grandmother Elmira had passed on by this time. I received a phone call from a lady — whom I'll call Bernice* — who was a very active member of the Rose of Sharon Church from way back. Her husband, however never attended services — and by this time they had become estranged.

"Reverend Joubert?"

"This is he."

"Reverend, this is Bernice from church. I need to see you as soon as possible."

"Are you troubled, Sister Bernice?"

"I have an urgent matter to discuss with you. I'll be there in about ten or fifteen minutes, Please don't disappoint me."

With that, she hung up. I could not imagine what was of such an urgent matter, but it was not long before I found out.

Bernice drove up in her car and blew her horn for me to come out to the car. When I stepped off the porch and got to her car she said, "Will you get in please and let's go for a ride? What I have to say will take a little time. While riding around I'll talk."

I replied, "Oh no, I can't take that chance of riding in a car with you alone." The fact is that this very stunning woman was so light-skinned, she could easily pass for white. I pointed this out to her. "A black man like me with you as white as you are? The police see me in a car with you, what you think will happen to

---

* Not her real name.

me?"

She said, "Don't worry about that. The chief of police and every other cop in this town knows me, and they know my car. I have an understanding with them, and they will not bother me."

Reluctantly, I got into her car.

As we drove, she said, "I have something to say to you that I have kept to myself too long."

"Which is…?"

"The truth is that I have been in love with you from day one to this day, and I want you to know it before you leave here again."

I don't have to tell you that her statement made me very nervous—and not a little bit conflicted inside.

I had her pull over. I got out and walked back to my sister's home. Bernice wasn't done yet, however. The next day she called again. "I'm glad I caught you at home," she said when I answered. "Now listen, I know your sister and husband have gone to work and you are there alone, I'll be there in fifteen minutes." And before I could register protest, she hung up.

Perhaps I should have made my escape—but I convinced myself that this woman was troubled and perhaps needed any spiritual help I could render.

"Spiritual" was not on the mind of the woman I saw come strutting up the road, wearing dark glasses and the most alluring dress she could find.

"A red-headed woman make a preacher Ball the Jack…"

It was Mary Magdalene, Queen Jezebel, and Bathsheba, all rolled into one package of simmering sexuality… Jesus, give me strength.

I opened the door when those shapely legs clad in silk stockings and dainty feet in French-heeled shoes stepped onto the porch. "Sister Bernice," I said as calmly as possible, "this is *not* a good idea—"

She placed her hands on those curvy hips, thrust her full bosom out at me, looked me straight in the eye, and said, "Samuel, you *better* open that door and let me in if you don't want me to make a scene out here."

I looked up and down the street nervously and decided—against my better judgment—to allow her in so as to avoid that scene.

I closed the door behind us. "Now, Sister Bernice, if you are troubled—"

"Shut up, Samuel!" Standing closer to me, she declared, "I'm here to prove to you that I am as much woman as you will ever need or want, and I'm not leaving until you give me that opportunity!"

Poor, beautiful Bernice... her loins afire with unrighteous lust... a lust that threatened to drag me down into Perdition.

She was, thankfully, not very persistent—or the good Lord was strong within me that day—or both. In any event, I was, with God's help, able to resist the temptation to give her "that opportunity." In due time, she left—and I breathed a sigh of relief and a prayer of thanksgiving.

After my return to New York, I received a long letter from Bernice along with a photograph. She wanted me to arrange a place for her in New York while the two of us spent a week together and made wedding arrangements.

This was one of those times that I was exceptionally grateful to be living in a pastor's home. I sought needed counsel from Reverend Williams.

Reverend Williams heard my story, read the letter, and looked at the photo, tapping his finger on the desk. He looked me straight in the eyes and asked, "Is this woman married or single?"

"As far as I know, she was married—but she and her husband are no longer together."

Reverend Williams nodded. "Well then, is she divorced from her husband?"

"I don't know."

Reverend Williams didn't mince words. "You have nothing to consider, Brother Joubert. Forget you ever met her." Leaning forward, he admonished me: "You must never forget who you are. You are a preacher of the Gospel of Jesus Christ. You must live the Gospel you preach." He stood, came around the desk, and laid a hand on my shoulder. "How could you stand in the pulpit and preach knowing that you took a man's wife from him?" Were she already divorced, he suggested, that would be a different story, but since as far as I knew she was still a married woman, any relationship outside of Christian fellowship was out of the question. "I repeat," said he, "you have nothing to consider—forget her."

That is exactly what I did.

Thanks be to God I have learned through experience and years of living that one must follow that admonition of Paul in 1 Thessalonians, 5:17: "pray unceasingly." Every day, study and meditate in God's word in order that you may overcome the many and varied temptations of this life.

There are times during which temptation comes in rapid successions.

In any secular employment I undertook outside of the ministry, I made it a personal rule not to get romantically involved when it came to the women with whom I worked.

Unfortunately, there were times when a woman couldn't take the hint. A few months after I had started working at Harlem Hospital, the man for whom I took over returned from the war and was naturally given back his old job. I was transferred to an operating room that ran twenty-four hours a day and given a choice of which shift I preferred. I agreed to work the night shift from midnight to 8 a.m.

Normally, it was just myself and a nurse on duty. Sometimes the "joint was jumping," and other times it was quiet. One night, the nurse I normally worked with called in sick, and a young student nurse was called in to cover her post. She was not as familiar with the various aspects of the work nor the locations of the various instruments and medications that had to be set up in the proper place for the patients being treated the next morning. Consequently she kept me with her whenever she went in the operating room. It seemed like she was to be afraid to be left alone.

One night, we were in the instrument closet together. This was a deep, but narrow room with shelves upon which operating instruments were stored. We had brought in a stretcher upon which we were to carry instruments to the autoclave for sterilization. With the stretcher in there, room to turn and maneuver was at a premium.

She was a woman of rare beauty with a shapely figure second to none. She pressed against me as she attempted to reach for the instruments on the higher shelves. I started to reach from behind her…

Suddenly, she wiggled around, and we found ourselves in each other's arms. Before I realized it, I was picking her up and helping her onto the stretcher, where she laid back, looked at me with half-closed eyes that said "take me now!" and started to unbutton her blouse.

If the Devil were indeed a hideous red monster with a tail, horns, and cloven hooves, it would be all too easy to resist him. I'm here to tell you that the Devil is a beautiful woman with a ripe, shapely figure and sensuous lips and smoldering bedroom eyes that will tempt you right into the burning pit of hell.

As I was about to give in, the good Lord called out to me: "Don't get involved! Stop while you are ahead! Don't forget your policy!" By the Grace of He who is my Rock and my Strength, I was able to pull back from the abyss.

Needless to say, this young student nurse was not happy. She became very angry at me and accused me of leading her on. She apparently spread some gossip about me to some of her friends, but I was never able to learn the exact nature of it.

She made one more attempt to seduce me on another night by asking me to prepare a stretcher on which she could lie down and sleep for awhile during her break—then said if the phone rang to come and get her. I helped her onto the stretcher—she'd taken off her shoes and unbuttoned her blouse again—but I turned around and left. I figured it was a trap and was not going to take any chances.

I had no interactions with her after that.

Road to the Altar

Meanwhile, my relationship with Edna—the governess working for the family on Park Avenue who'd slipped whiskey into my ginger ale—had heated up to the point at which we became engaged to be married. Her beauty and her sexy ways had my head spinning—surely this is what Sampson had to contend with when Delilah put the moves on him.

But I was also getting to know Doris—slowly, gradually. Before I moved out of the YMCA to live with Pastor Williams, Doris would find excuses to come by. I never had her in my room, but the desk clerk would let her ring me sometimes. Often, when I went to the dining room around 11 p.m. to grab a meal before heading to my shift at the hospital, she would sit with me and watch me eat.

I wasn't quite sure what to make of Doris at first. I actually met her father one evening. Mr. Thorpe worked as a chef in the dining car on a passenger run between New York City and Miami. He was gone for five days and home for two. He was hard to read, and I was never certain if he was impressed with me or not.

My engagement to Edna was a troubled one. In retrospect, that stunt with the whiskey in my ginger ale should have been a red flag, but "love (or at least lust) is blind." It also didn't help that I was seeing not one, but *three* young ladies at the time—Edna, Doris, and one whom I'll call Peggy*. As you might imagine, me working with the Shadows of Gethsemane Gospel Choir and preaching and singing at so many churches—and being a man that women found attractive—I had many an opportunity to meet equally attractive young ladies.

"It is better to marry than to burn." So wrote the apostle Paul in his first letter to the Corinthians. I was now going on twenty-six years of age. It was about this time—when I was juggling relationships with Edna, Doris, and Peggy—that the Lord spoke to me: "Samuel, it is high time you settle down in marriage. Your future success will be predicated upon your prayerful choice of your life's mate now. You can't have all three—you can only have one, and it must be in marriage, if you want My Blessing. No ifs, ands, or buts about it."

I prayed over this matter most intently. By this time, I had earned about a month's vacation time from the hospital, and decided that what I needed to do was go home to Louisiana for a spell. One of the women I worked with was from New Orleans, and when she found out that I was going home, she asked me if I would stop and visit her parents—apparently assuming that the Crescent City was my destination.

I was about to tell her that my home town where I was headed was well over a hundred miles from New Orleans and I'd made no plans to go anywhere else when something inside me said, *Don't.* I agreed to take her parents' phone number and told her I would try to

---

* Not her real name.

contact them for her if I could.

About a month before I left for home, I had a dream in which a voice said, "Don't go back the way you came."

I woke up with that voice still in my head. *Don't go back the way you came.*

It finally dawned on me what that meant. Normally, I traveled on the Penn Central west and changed trains in Chicago, then traveled south by a route that took me into Alexandria. This time however, the Lord wanted me to go by way of New Orleans.

This time, I arranged to ride the Penn Central to Chicago then pick up the *Panama Limited* on the Illinois Central. Once I got to New Orleans, I'd hop the local that went through Baton Rouge and ended up in Opelousas. What happened however is that the *Panama* on that trip wound up stopping several miles short of the New Orleans terminal. I looked at my watch—there was only thirty minutes left if I was to make my connection to Opelousas.

I stopped one of the porters. "What's the trouble?"

He replied, "Couplin's broke—we gotta wait 'til the maintenance people can bring a new one."

By the time the repair was completed and our train had reached New Orleans, my connection was long gone. According to the ticket agent, there would not be another train to Opelousas until the next day.

Trying to decide if I should find a hotel room somewhere nearby, I remembered the phone number that the young woman had given me. I decided to give her parents a call.

She had told them to expect me; they received me

with open arms.

I ended up staying in New Orleans for two weeks. They were among the most eventful two weeks of my life. The lady of the house was an evangelist preacher and made a few phone calls, making several preaching engagements for me. She also had an interesting friend to whom I was introduced.

I hadn't met anyone like Angelique* before—and I haven't since. She was as dark and beautiful as a Nubian princess—but more importantly, she radiated an incredible spiritual presence. Being in the same room with her, you knew you were in the presence of a mighty servant of God.

During my time in New Orleans, she held services in her home. Afterwards, she took me aside.

"You have a great future ahead of you," Angelique said to me. "I see you standing in the pulpit of a church, of which you will be the pastor, praising the Lord for His bountiful blessings to you." Then, she added, "You will be blessed with a number of children of which you will be very proud. One boy will be really special—and if I were you, I would call him 'Joseph.'"

She then told me of my love life and warned me of some pitfalls I would do well to avoid.

When I left New Orleans much of what had been unclear to me in regard to choosing the right mate had become as clear as a sunlit day. I knew what I had to do; my mind was made up.

After spending the third week with my parents in Grand Prairie and the fourth week with my sister Clara

---

* Not her real name.

and her husband in Alexandria, I returned to New York, and I prayerfully and peacefully cancelled my engagement with Edna.

Doris and I had a number of occasions to spend some time together walking in Mount Morris Park and sitting on the bench and enjoying looking at the beautiful scenery. It was while sitting on a bench in Mount Morris Park that I made my proposal.

"Doris," I said, "I love you and want to marry you if you will have me as your husband with this understanding: I am not interested in a career wife. I want a wife who will be the mother of our children and who will be home and help bring them up right. No wife of mine will have to work outside the home once the marriage vows are taken.

"I will become responsible for all your needs. I understand you like music and singing. You can use your musical talent working in the church with me. It is your decision to make."

It didn't take her long. She agreed to marry me right then and there.

Chapter IX
Married, with Children — and a Church

Therefore a man leaves his father and his mother and cleaves to his wife, and they become one flesh.
—Genesis 2:24

Marriage according to the scripture is a divine institution instituted by God Almighty Himself. No couple should get married without having prayed about choosing a mate and been sufficiently counseled by a spiritually and morally strong God-fearing experienced pastor—and it doesn't hurt to be in good with your prospective in-laws, either.

A Rocky Start

Not everyone was as joyous about our impending union as Doris and I.

A few days later she went to the music studio where she was taking singing lessons. She told her teacher she would not be continuing, because she had decided that a happy Christian marriage was more important to her then a venture in the pursuit of a singing career.

That very night her father called me around 1 a.m. while I was on the job at Harlem Hospital. He was furious. "On whose authority do you advise my daughter to change her mind about her musical career?" he demanded.

My reply was, "Sir, she is your daughter and the lady I hope to marry, and she is too important to discuss on the telephone. This matter should be discussed in person." I told him that I would be happy to come by his place when I got off work and we could talk about it.

I arrived around 8:30 the next morning. Doris' father was still angry, but as King Solomon the Wise said, "a soft answer turneth away wrath" (Proverbs 15:1). I explained to Mr. Thorpe that I would never interfere in his relationship with his daughter, but if she would have me, I was prepared to be her husband in every sense of that word.

Before my decision to settle down and take a wife, I'd had (as you know from reading this far) one other unfortunate trait in common with King Solomon. I had in my young life "loved many strange women." Now, this would no longer be an issue—I would cleave unto Doris for the rest of our days together, and there was nothing about her that was strange, only that which was wondrous—but I had a few loose ends to tie up.

The first of these had been Edna. She of course was not happy about my ending our engagement, but she accepted it with grace and class. Peggy was another matter. I can never forget that pitiful scene. It was worse than I had anticipated. She cried almost uncontrollably, and she almost had me crying.

"Samuel," she cried when I told her about my impending marriage, "I have a good job! You won't have to work—I'll take care of you while you're in school, just as long as you'll promise to marry me!"

It was the worst argument she could have made. I could never let a woman or anyone else support me as long as I had health and strength. I would by the help of God foot my own bills.

Next she blamed herself, begging to know what she'd done wrong. I tried to explain that it had nothing to do with her. Finally, she demanded to know what hold Doris had over me. The decision was mine, I said.

"Heav'n hath no Rage, like Love to Hatred turn'd—nor Hell a Fury like a Woman scorned." The poet who penned that line three hundred years ago must have looked into the future and seen Peggy as I ended our relationship. As I look back over that scene, I thank the Lord she was a Christian woman. Otherwise I may not have left her place alive.

I am pleased to report that some years later, she met and married a fine man who was also a preacher and bore him several children. She had by that time forgiven me, and she and her family came to worship at the church where I eventually become pastor.

There was one last matter to deal with—one about which I had not even been aware.

For better or worse, a man is judged by the company he keeps. It was my landlord and counselor, Reverend Williams, who brought the matter to my attention. Shortly after I had placed Doris' engagement ring on her finger, I was passing Reverend Williams' study on my way up to my room. He stepped out.

"Brother Joubert, could I speak with you for a moment?"

I stepped into his study. He motioned to one of the leather chairs in front of his desk. "Joubert, have a seat."

"Is there a problem, Reverend?" I asked, somewhat concerned by his grave tone of voice.

He sat down behind his desk, folding his hands before him. "Brother Joubert, Rosemary [Mrs. Williams] has been after me to talk to you, because she feels as if you were our own son."

I nodded, swallowing. Reverend Williams continued: "You've been going around with this preacher Salisberry."

"Yes sir—I count him as my friend and colleague," I answered.

Reverend Williams nodded. "We know him better than you do," he said. "He drinks alcohol and runs with any and all women he can persuade." This came as a total shock to me. Either I hadn't seen this side of my friend—or, as was more likely, I had *chosen* not to see it. Reverend Williams stood up, came around, and put a hand on my shoulder. "Son, we know this is not your character. We know you don't drink or smoke or chase skirts as Salisberry does. We believe, however, that it would be best for your future marriage and career in the ministry if you were to cut off your relationship with him before people start looking upon you as they do him."

Despite my great affection for Reverend Salisberry, I knew that Reverend Williams was a conscientious, ethical, and highly moral man who would not have told me such a thing had it not been true. I took him at his word and ended my association with Reverend

Salisberry.

It had been none too soon. Less than six months later, Salisberry was expelled from his church for making advances toward a sixteen-year-old girl.

I learned this lesson as a young preacher: One must be extremely careful in taking someone into one's inner circle simply because he or she can sing, pray, and preach. One must make certain the individual has good moral principles and is a trustworthy, honest, born-again, God-fearing Christian.

Our Wedding Day

It was bright and sunny the day I wed my darling Doris on the eleventh day of September, 1948. We were married at the Cosmopolitan Baptist Church; Reverend Williams had secured two or three policemen to control the traffic and parking around the church.

The wedding took place in the main sanctuary, which was filled with friends and loved ones. My cousin Matthew served as my best man, and Reverend Williams himself performed the ceremony.

After we all went down to the church dining room for a lovely reception, we went to a picture studio a few blocks away to have our wedding pictures taken.

As I was now a married man with a wife, Reverend Williams allowed me to rent the entire top floor apartment, which included a kitchen, a bedroom and bath, and a living room as well as the small room off the hall where I had been living. When the reception was over, we walked upstairs to that apartment, where I carried Doris over the threshold, into the living room, and finally the bedroom, where we spent our blissful wedding night.

Word Gets Around

A few days after my wedding, upon reporting for my shift at Harlem Hospital, the nurse who worked the night shift with me in the operating room greeted me with gloom and hope.

"Why didn't you tell us you were getting married?"

I said, "who said I got married?"

She answered, "The old nurse on 3 West was at your wedding and told the nurse on 5 South about it, and *she* told *me*."

I told her that I thought I would keep it a secret for a while. I did not want to upset my co-workers. She shocked me by saying, "Reverend, all of us here thought perhaps you did not like women because you never showed any interest in us romantically. Now that we know you like women, your stock is going up!"

A warning to married men: "beware." Always remember your marriage vows. The Devil never lets up on temptation.

Word soon got around to the rest of my immediate co-workers, and they insisted on coming over to meet my new bride. We arranged a small reception for them at our apartment, and they came bearing gifts and good wishes—but mainly to see what my new bride looked like. Doris treated them with love and respect; she was an excellent hostess, and my co-workers all seemed to have been impressed.

Several months after my marriage, I got word that Edna, my ex-fiancée, had been in a subway accident and had lost a leg. She had been brought to Harlem Hospital and was requesting that I come see her.

I had mixed feeling about this, and as usual, sought the counsel of Reverend Williams. I thought surely he would agree that I should visit her and pray with her.

To my surprise, he replied by quoting Romans 14:16—"Let not then your good be evil spoken of." He explained that while he had no doubt that my intentions were good and honorable, my visiting one with whom I had been so intimate with could be misconstrued: "This is one case in which your good deed could be evil spoken of," he said. "My advice is to stay away."

I took the reverend's words to heart and did not have any contact with Edna.

It was about four years later, after Doris and I had moved to the St. Nicholas Projects on Eighth Avenue and 131st Street. I was sitting on a bench outside our building, waiting for a bus, when a lady on crutches, wearing a wooden leg and accompanied by a little girl about two or three years old, came by.

It was Edna. She had come to visit a friend who lived in the building.

I saw Edna in passing perhaps twice more after that. Then one night, I received a phone call from her.

"Sam?"

"Edna... what's up?"

"Sam, I know that I have caused you some worry and problems over the years. I promise you that I will never be any more problem or worry to you, ever. I am leaving for Switzerland and will be out of your life for good."

"The Lord watch over you and yours, Sister Edna," I said.

"Thank you, Sam. God bless."

That was our conversation. I have not seen nor heard from Edna since, but pray she found some peace in her life.

Home To Meet the Family

In late December of 1948, I decided to take my wife with me to meet my parents and other relatives and friends in Louisiana.

We left NYC a few days after Christmas while a snowstorm was at its peak. We secured a roomette on the train and had a nice, belated honeymoon trip all the way to Louisiana. On arriving at my parents' home in Grand Prairie, Louisiana, we were greeted with open arms. My mother and father fell in love with Doris almost at first sight.

As was the tradition at my home I took my new wife around with me to visit and be introduced to my extended family. Since it was between Christmas and New Year's, everywhere we went we were served cake or pie and table wine.

After spending a week with my parents and relatives around Grand Prairie and Opelousas, we went to Alexandria. Clara received us with open arms. Doris and my sister Clara hit if off right away and got along very well.

After a week stay in Alexandria, we boarded the

train back to NYC.

My In-Laws

Not too long after we were married, my father-in-law, George—who had been less than friendly—suddenly called on us for help. His youngest child, George Thorpe Jr., was in high school and had been failing in his subjects. At the time, he was enrolled in a private school in Pennsylvania; he could not live at home with his father because George Sr. spent most of his time traveling on the railroad in the course of his employment. George Sr.'s older daughter, Geraldine, was in college in North Carolina.

He had no one else to appeal to for help but us. The small room off the hall in which I had stayed before marrying Doris remained vacant at the time, so we consented to take him in. We fixed him up a bed in that room, and he came to live with us, enrolling in Washington Heights High School.

George was a real trip. He would always take his bath in the tub and go to sleep with the water up to his neck. I cannot count the times I had to wake him up and make him get out of the tub and go to bed. He chose the wrong crowd to pal around with and was always coming in at really late hours. He was difficult to discipline. Our relief came when he went into the army and was sent to Germany.

The next occupant of that room was Doris' sister, Geraldine. By the time George Jr. went off to boot camp, Geraldine had graduated from college. She came to live with us while working as a lab technician over at Presbyterian Hospital.

She was also instrumental in the founding of the church of which I would become a full-fledged pastor. The New Jerusalem Baptist Church which got its start with my leadership was then in an embryonic state. Geraldine became a chartered member and served as clerk of the new church. She was faithful and dependable and kept excellent accurate records. But that was later.

Our Firstborn

In the summer of 1949, Doris and I had not been married a year when she announced she was expecting. Around 2:30 on the morning of March 18, 1950, I was awakened by a phone call from the maternity ward of Harlem Hospital, informing me that my wife had given birth to a frail son weighing less than five pounds. He was not expected to live; the chaplain had been called to for pray for the child.

I immediately got dressed and made my way to the hospital and got my first look at our firstborn, Samuel B. Joubert Jr. For the first few days his new life hung in the balance, because he showed no interest in being fed.

Fortunately, there was an older nurse with much experience with such cases. Upon finding out whose child he was, she made it her business to care for him personally. She used an old folk remedy and mixed a little whiskey into his milk bottle.

That whiskey turned the tide. He took to drinking his milk and eating with a great appetite. From then on

Married With Children – and a Church

he began to gain strength and put on weight. After a week or more we were allowed to bring him home, although he was kept under a great deal of doctor's care. He grew nicely, however, and became a handsome, bouncing baby boy.

I was still employed at the Harlem Hospital, working the nightshift, and did my sleeping during the day. By the time Samuel Jr. had begun to crawl, I took to placing him in his crib with high sides and ends to keep him from falling out. One day, Doris was out, so I made certain that he was fast asleep and could not get out of the crib.

I lay down to take a nap. I had not been asleep more than thirty minutes when a loud voice spoke to me saying, *"Wake up!"* When I woke up, the first thing I did was to see about the baby in the crib; and the crib was empty. I frantically looked all over the house—no baby. Then I looked to the window; it was open, and on the ledge was little Samuel, crawling towards the end—seven floors above the pavement!

I quickly and quietly got on to the ledge, reached our son and pulled him back to safety just in time. How a crawling baby got out the crib with high sides and up to the window and onto the ledge is beyond me. I can only say "Praise God!" for watching over me and my son. It pays to know the Lord and be in constant communication with Him.

Our Second Born

Our second son, David Eugene Joubert, was born on May 16, 1952. When Doris started having contractions, we called for an ambulance, which started taking us to a private hospital. We wanted to go to Harlem Hospital, and it took a great deal of arguing with the driver to convince him to change his destination.

David Eugene was in a hurry to come into the world—he popped out of his mama's womb thirty minutes after we arrived at the maternity ward. He weighed eight pounds and was a healthy boy with fair skin like his grandmother.

Up until then, Samuel Jr. had been a happy, bubbling over with joy, playful baby. But when a second child was bought home he changed suddenly and was less playful and happy. Eventually he did adjust to the fact that there was another child who was in the household to stay and not a visitor.

Our Third Child: Deborah

On the morning of April 20, 1954, around 2:30 a.m., I received a phone call from the nurse on duty at Harlem Hospital on the maternity ward, who reported that I was now the father of a beautiful baby girl weighing a little more than seven pounds.

I got dressed in a hurry and left Samuel Jr. and David with their aunt Geraldine. On arrival at the hospital I was permitted to see my beautiful daughter, a charming light brown baby—Deborah Elizabeth Joubert.

A few days later this proud father brought his wife and baby daughter home. Later on that day Reverend Williams came upstairs to see our new baby girl. He looked at Samuel Jr. and he looked at David, then he took another look at Deborah and said, "These boys are nice looking, but this baby is beautiful! Brother Joubert, you struck oil this time."

The New Jerusalem Church

David Eugene was not the only joyful arrival for us in 1952: it was also the year that New Jerusalem was recognized as an independent church by the General Baptist Association.

On September 23, 1952, we started meeting in a building just off Amsterdam Ave at 423 West 156th Street. Daisy Littlejohn and her sister, two of our charter members, lived just across the street. They would clean the church and set everything in order for Sunday services the day before, donating their time and labor. Sister Daisy's daughter-in-law furnished the flowers for the church at no cost. She was also a concert artist, and performed at many benefit concerts for our church.

The New Jerusalem Baptist Church was formally incorporated October 7, 1952.

Meanwhile, I was still employed at Harlem Hospital. On a number of occasions, I had told my members that God was telling me it was time for me to become a full-time pastor, devoting all my energies to the care of the flock.

I will never forget one particular Sunday when I preached on the subject "Faith in God will make the impossible, possible." By that time, my preaching ability had matured, and I felt very good about the sermon. The first member of the flock to come and shake my hands was Sister Daisy Littlejohn.

She grabbed my hand and held it tight, then looked me straight in the eye and said, "What a powerful message… but you don't believe it yourself!!!"

"What…?"

"You have stood in that same pulpit and told us that the Lord told *you* He wanted all of your time in the ministry of the Word."

"That is true, Sister Daisy—"

"But you *haven't* quit that job, yet!"

Her words hit me like a ton of bricks. You better believe I truly prayed to the Lord about the matter of quitting my job, because at the time I had two little children with another one on the way, and the small congregation was not prepared to take care of all my expenses.

One night not long after this, I had a dream in which I saw my wife and children out in the suburb with a large beautiful tablecloth, spread on green grass, loaded with every kind of dish of food and fruits you could name.

I said to my wife, "Honey, where did you get all of that food?"

She answered, "The Lord gave it to us."

The next morning, I spoke to my wife and said, "The Lord just gave the answer to my prayer."

Several days later, I walked onto the office of the chief administrator at Harlem Hospital and told the person in charge that I was resigning from my position. She looked at me almost in shock and said, "What are you going to do for a living?"

Married With Children – and a Church

I replied, "I'm going to preach the Gospel and live by the Gospel." That was in 1954; I was thirty-two years old.

Since that time, I have spent all my energies preaching the Word of God and caring for His flock. I have been a licensed pastor in the state of New York for fifty-two years.

After the birth of Deborah, it would be four years before another child arrived. Those four years nonetheless would prove to be eventful and challenging ones.

Chapter X
Raising a Family, Leading a Flock

Now that we had had three children, our residence over Pastor William's church had become too small.

We filled out several applications for new projects being built. We finally received notice in 1956 that we were accepted to receive a two-bedroom apartment with living room, kitchen, and bath in the St. Nicholas Housing Project on 131st Street and Eighth Avenue. Just before we relocated, we secured a place for Geraldine at the YWCA, near where I had first stayed upon my arrival in NYC ten years earlier. It was a bittersweet occasion for the children, as Samuel, David, and Deborah had become closely attached to their aunt Geraldine.

Pastoral Problems

After worshipping in our new church home for a while, we decided to get new and better chairs. I went downtown and decided on some folding, theater-style chairs, attached in rows of five or more, that I felt would best meet our need. I signed the contract for the folding chairs.

The truckload was delivered on a Saturday. As they were being unloaded, I noticed a number of rows with one or more chairs missing. I immediately stopped them from unloading the chairs and instructed them to put all the chairs back on the truck because I was not about to accept chairs that did not measure up to what I was shown.

To my surprise, I received a phone call early the following Monday morning during which I was informed that according to the contract, I was obligated to accept the chairs, and they were being returned to me. I pondered over the matter for a while and decided to seek advice from my old friend Reverend G. C. Williams.

He asked me to read the contract to him, which I did. He paused for a moment then said, "Joubert, you have to accept those chairs. The contract obligates you to do so."

"But these weren't the chairs I was shown!" I protested.

Reverend Williams replied, "You have one recourse—go there and bluff your way through this situation."

I went to the office and said to the merchant, "Suppose we were in court and the judge asked me to explain my action? I would be forced to tell him that you showed me a row of attached folding chairs with none missing, otherwise… I would not have signed any contract for rows with missing chairs." Then, looking him straight in the eye, I said, "What do you think the judge would do?"

The fact is, this was a case of *caveat emptor*. I should have demanded to see the exact chairs I was receiving before I'd signed anything, and then watched them being loaded. In fact, in a court of law, it would have been my word against his.

He fell for the bluff and said, "Here is what I'm going to do. I am going to give you plywood to fill in all missing chairs, and I will include some extra plywood and chairs." I agreed to this compromise; the delivery was made with all the plywood we needed and then some, along with extra chairs.

The matter of the chairs caused some other problems as well. Shortly after this, our annual financial report was given. Sister Littlejohn, who raised the most money for the building fund, became annoyed and said that too much money had been spent on chairs and a few other items. She proceeded to stand up and walk out of the meeting in protest, calling on her sister to follow her.

I remember the occasion as if it were yesterday. I spoke to her in a low tone of voice. "Don't you walk out of that door." She kept on walking. I repeated, "Sister Littlejohn, did you hear what I said? Don't walk out of that door." She ignored my plea and walked out and went home and took her sister with her.

Several weeks later her sister called me and informed me that her sister was in Lincoln's Hospital in the Bronx. Would I go and pray for her? I complied with her request. After a week in the hospital she was sent home. God was kind and allowed Sister Littlejohn to worship with us one last time. After that, the legs and feet on which she had stormed out of the church gave out on her and shriveled up, causing her to be unable to walk for the rest of her life. Despite our disagreement, she loved me and I loved her; our friendship never ceased. When the Lord finally called her home, I preached at her funeral and went all the way to the cemetery to see her laid to rest.

Associate Pastor Problems

During our time living at St. Nicholas Project, there was a cleaning shop nearby on Eighth Avenue to which I took my suits for cleaning and pressing. A lady who worked there had occasion to talk to me about religion. Naturally, I directed her to the New Jerusalem Baptist Church. She came to worship one Sunday and eventually joined as a member.

One day, she said to me, "I have a brother who is a young preacher and is coming to New York. I want him to meet you." This brother, whom I'll call Simon*, turned out to be a handsome man around twenty-nine to thirty years old. He joined us at New Jerusalem, where I made him my associate pastor. Brother Simon proved to be very helpful. He drove a nice car, and since I did not own an automobile at the time, he was nice enough to drive my family and me wherever we wanted to go. He visited our home and took meals with us on a number of occasions.

At the same time, there was a young beautiful lady in our church named Louella*. She had a lovely personality and was dedicated and loyal. She was the most influential person in her family; after becoming a member of New Jerusalem, she brought in her whole family, including her mother, father, sisters, brothers, nieces and nephews, friends, and in-laws.

---

* Not his real name.
* Also not her real name.

Raising an Family, Leading a Flock

One day, she called me really upset and crying. "Brother Pastor," she said, "I am at my wits' end, and I need you to come and pray with me as I don't want to have to kill somebody."

"Can you tell me more?" I asked.

"I don't want to talk about it on the phone," she said. "Just come as soon as you can, and I will explain."

For reasons of which my reader is well aware, I was at first hesitant to go. Nonetheless, the Spirit said to me, "Go on, Sam—help this poor soul. You can deal with it."

When I arrived at Louella's home, she invited me in and we sat in the living room. Her eyes red from crying, she said, "Brother Pastor, this nigger told me he was not married and had divorced his wife!"

Calmly, I asked, "Who is this man?"

"Brother Simon!" she spat. She confessed that he had been sleeping with her. "Then today he calls me and tells me he has to go to the airport and pick up his wife!" At this, she broke down crying again.

We prayed together there in her living room. Before leaving, I gave her some scripture references to study and upon which I felt she would do well to meditate. "Don't do anything foolish in this moment of distress, Sister Louella," I admonished her. "Pray, meditate on the Word, and wait on God for strength and guidance to carry you through these turbulent times."

When I confronted Brother Simon on the issue, he bowed his head in shame. I told him that under the circumstances I could not have him sit in the pulpit with me, particularly with Louella and her family sitting in the audience knowing what he had done. Naturally, he left New Jerusalem and eventually New York itself.

Sadly, Louella was never the same afterwards. She lost her zeal and her passion for worship.

The Problem of Pain

At this point, I am going to interrupt this narrative of my life, because I would like to share some of my thoughts on the subject of pain and the trials through which the Almighty God puts us through over the course of our lives.

While I do not judge Sister Louella and those like her whose faith is shaken and even lost due to such trials, I will say here and now for the record that such pain can strengthen our faith as well. Like many of us, I have experienced the loss of a loved one, sickness, disappointments, and betrayal.

One of the mistakes a Christian makes when faced with tragedy and pain is to blame God. Either God caused it, or God allowed it to happen. While this reaction is understandable, it is a wrong impression. The great English writer and Christian apologist C. S. Lewis got it right when he wrote that nearly all the pain humans experience is caused not by God, but by other humans.

God did not send Simon to seduce and betray Louella, nor did God force Louella to take Simon into her bed. All parties involved had free will in the matter. Simon knew he was violating his marriage vows, but blinded by lust, he failed to see the consequences. Louella (and forgive me, but sometimes I wonder if it wasn't Adam that offered the fruit to Eve) also had a choice of not succumbing to Simon's charms before she had come to know him better.

My paternal grandmother, Florestine, was made a widow when a highway robber waylaid my grandfather Edmond on his way back from selling his cotton one year. The man who shot my grandfather dead for thirteen cents was not sent by God. He made a choice, and Grandmother Florestine lost her husband because of it.

One of the most monstrous examples of human cruelty that I know of occurred when a great man with whom I had the privilege to work one time was allowed to die for no other reason than the color of his skin. Dr. Charles Drew was a great African-American physician who came to us at Harlem Hospital one night during my time there to demonstrate the nature and use of something he himself had discovered, which has saved millions of lives: blood plasma. Yet only months later, he was traveling through the South and was injured in an automobile accident. A blood transfusion—the basis of which he himself had discovered and shared with the world—would have saved him, but the nearest hospital was for "Whites Only."

Again, God was not at fault here. It was the ignorance and bigotry of humans that caused the death of this kind and brilliant man of science.

My uncle Leon was killed at a railroad crossing when he panicked behind the wheel of his Model T, pushing down on the wrong pedal and causing the vehicle to leap ahead and into the path of the train that killed him. He had been a fine deacon and an excellent father. Yet, can we blame God for such a loss? Or had Uncle Leon, bless his memory, been responsible for his own demise by failing to take proper precautions?

Yes, Pastor Joubert, I can hear you saying—but what of illness and accident? What of fire, flood and other natural disasters? Are those not acts of God?

This is a challenging question. It is true that my little brother and sister, Edmo and Ruthie, did not choose to catch the pneumonia that took them away at such a tender age. In retrospect, all I can say is that perhaps those two precious children were too good for this world. Just as Reverend White had told the late Pastor White's congregation that he needed me by his side, so too did the Lord choose to call Edmo and Ruthie home early on, sparing them the trials and tribulations of this life.

You recall Marcia, the young Catholic lady from New Orleans whom I had known in Alexandria and with whom I had seriously considered joining in marriage at one point. As you know, despite the different views we held regarding the path to Heaven, we remained close friends and continued to correspond for many years.

Sometime before I met Doris, I received a letter from Marcia in which she reported that a young man she had been dating had asked her to marry him. I suppose that hoping there was still some small chance for the two of us, she wanted to know where I stood before giving this man her answer.

If you listen to that "still, small voice" within,

you'll find that God indeed does His level best to lead us through the shadows of the Valley of Death. That small, still voice told me not to respond to that letter. Shortly afterward, I received an announcement of her impending wedding.

Whatever success and safety I have enjoyed in this life is due to the fact that God has granted me visions along the way, and I allow myself to be led by these visions. In my vision of Marcia's wedding, which came in a dream, a Voice spoke to me, clearly saying: "If she goes through with this marriage, it will end with her tragic death."

I woke up trembling. I pondered and pondered over this dream. Should I warn her of the dream or not? I finally came to the conclusion that it would be most impractical for me to interfere with her plans for marriage at this juncture.

It was not until many years later that I learned of Marcia's fate. In 1951, she and her husband were living in Baton Rouge, and she was returning home from Alexandria aboard the *Southern Belle,* a passenger train that ran through central Louisiana on its way between Kansas City and New Orleans. It was a modern streamliner, one that I had ridden on many occasions.

On August 10 of that year, the southbound train on which Marcia was riding collided head-on with a military troop train on its way to Alexandria. It was the worst railroad accident in the history of the L&A Railroad; Marcia was among the thirteen passengers that were killed.

Marcia was a dear friend of whom I cherished very much. She went to be with the Lord in a tragic accident. Should I have warned her? Was her death my fault? Or had the Lord, through that dream, simply been warning me so that I might be prepared?

Whatever the hurt or tragedy we suffer, whether (as is most often the case) it is at the hands of other humans, or if it appears to be what even insurance companies call "Acts of God," it is natural for us to ask, "Why?"

I cannot speak for others, but I can tell you that in times of such pain and trouble. I find comfort in the words of the Apostle Paul in 2 Corinthians 12,7–10:

> *To keep me from becoming conceited because of these surpassingly great revelations, there was given me a thorn in my flesh, a messenger of Satan to torment me. Three times I pleaded with the Lord to take it away from me. But He said to me 'My grace is sufficient for you, for my power is made perfect in weakness.' Therefore I will boast all the more gladly about my weakness, so that Christ's power may rest on me. That is why for Christ's sake, I delight in weakness, in insults, in hardships, in persecutions, in difficulties. For when I am weak, then I am strong.*

Our human weakness, afflictions, and serious problems provide the ideal opportunity for the display of the divine power of God to comfort and sustain us if we have sense enough to call on Him by faith. Now consider Job 1:18–22:

> *While he was still speaking, yet, another*

> *messenger came and said, 'Your sons and daughters were feasting and drinking wine at the oldest brother's house, when suddenly a mighty wind swept in from the desert and struck the four corner of the house. It collapsed on them and they are dead and I am the only one who has escaped to tell you.' At this Job got up and tore his robe and shaved his head. Then he fell to the ground in worship and said: Naked I came from my mother's womb and naked I will depart. The Lord gave and the Lord has taken away; blessed be the Name of the Lord.*

In all this, Job did not sin by charging God with wrongdoing. Job's faith led him to see the sovereign God's hand at work; that gave him peace of mind and freedom from worrying in the face of calamity. Good men will not overlook God's hand when calamities come upon them, nor fail to humble themselves before him.

Nothing so sustains the soul in the day of severe trial and sudden calamities as the knowledge that God "is our refuge and underneath are His everlasting arms" (Deuteronomy 33:27); "Yea, God is our refuge and strength, a very present help in trouble" (Psalm 46:1). He is, as Moses wrote, "our dwelling place throughout all generations" (Psalm 90:1).

The presence and favor of God are at all times the security, support and comfort for those who put their trust in Him. As God dealt with Job so will he deal with us today when we exercise the same amount of faith as Job did. One must always remember that suffering can be redemptive.

Tragedy, sickness, and death are a part of this life, and no one is exempted. Likewise joy, happiness, and prosperity are also a part of this existence. Life can be beautiful and meaningful if you live it by faith in Christ today, doubting nothing.

Our Fourth Child

Through tragedies and setbacks, the Lord continued to bless our family. Four years after Deborah was born, my wife again conceived.

She let me know by knitting baby clothes, which I noticed were for a girl child. When I asked her about it, she indicated she was expecting and hoping for another girl.

I then remembered what Angelique had told me in New Orleans many years before, when I finally came to the knowledge that Doris was the life-partner and help-mate God had intended for me:

> "You will be blessed with a number of children of which you will be very proud. One boy will be really special…"

Remembering that remarkable woman's advice, I said to Doris, "Forget about another girl. This child is a boy, and his name is Joseph."

On July 7, 1958, Doris told me it was time to go to the hospital. I got us a taxi, and we went to Harlem Hospital; not long after arrival there our fourth child was born. Joseph Edward Joubert came into this world healthy and happy at eight pounds and twelve ounces.

I saw on his forehead the mark of someone special.

My Masonic Affiliation

I had been first initiated into the fraternal order of Masons in 1948. By 1956 I was serving as Grand Secretary of the Most Worshipful Alpha Grand Lodge A. F. & A. M., where the Rev. G. C. Williams was Grand Master. I was also Grand Secretary of the Consistory.

In 1958 our United Supreme Council met in Los Angeles California. I was scheduled to preach during the religious service for this bi-annual conference. It was an informative, exciting, and historical session. I was elected to the office of Grand Chancellor, the fourth highest office in the Supreme Council.

During one of our Masonic meetings about a year later, G. C. Williams announced that I was to be elevated to the position of Grand Prior—third man in the Kingdom.

I replied, "How can that be?" I had held the office of Grand Chancellor only a short time.

He answered, "Don't question me. The Grand Prior recently died, and you, Reverend Samuel B. Joubert, have been elevated to his position."

This was not to be the last promotion for me, however. Some time later the Lieutenant Commander was removed for insubordination. Reverend Williams—who was ill at the time—came to see me on a Sunday afternoon at New Jerusalem Baptist Church. After the conclusion of the service, he met with me in my office.

"Joubert, I am pondering over who I will appoint to fill the vacancy of the position of Lieutenant Commander," he said. "There are several brothers who are older than you and know more about the order than you because of their age and experience. However," he added, "you have greater leadership ability then they."

He then gave me a solemn look. "Should I choose to appoint you, can I trust that you will you carry out the work and follow the landmarks as I have taught you?"

"Certainly, I would," I replied. He left, relieved and satisfied that I was as good as my word. However, as fate would have it, my dear friend and mentor passed on before he could make the appointment.

The death of Reverend G. C. Williams and the dismissal of the Lieutenant Commander left the Supreme Council with its two top positions vacant. To complicate matters, an older member—whose name was also Williams and who had been a friend and colleague of the Reverend G. C. much longer then I—had quickly gone to his widow and told her he should succeed her husband. G. C.'s widow, Rosemary, gave him the papers and all that goes with the office.

At first, I did not protest this action and accepted this M. C. Williams' claim on Reverend G. C.'s former office. However, a little later, my old friend came to me in a vision and said. "I want you to succeed me." With a gesture of his right hand, he said, "Fight for it!"

I immediately began to read the Constitution and Bylaws of the Council as well as any and all literature I could find on the election of officers. Nonetheless, I could not find anything to justify my taking over as Sovereign Grand Commander, even though I was the highest living elected officer. The Constitution was very clear on this point: in order to be elected to office of Sovereign Grand Commander, one must first have served as Lieutenant Commander—which I had not.

I pondered over this matter and was about to give up, when suddenly it came to me as a light in the darkness. This was not to be an election; this unusual situation *demanded* succession. Though I had not held the office of Lieutenant Commander, I was nonetheless the highest surviving office holder.

I called a meeting of all the men of the 33rd Degree and said to them: "In the line of succession I currently hold the highest office in the Supreme Council. In light of this unusual situation, I am as of this moment assuming the office of Sovereign Grand Commander of the United Supreme Council." With one stroke of the gavel I assumed the position. Then I had M. C. Williams turn over to me all that he had acquired from Reverend G. C.'s widow and went forward with the work of the council.

In order to heal any divisions, I appointed M. C. Williams as my Lieutenant Commander.

As Sovereign Grand Commander, I attended the meeting of the Federation of Masons of the World in Detroit, Michigan, in 1964 and was elected Fifth Vice President of the Federation. In 1967, I again attended the meeting of the Federation of Masons of the World in San Antonio, Texas, at which I was elected Grand Chaplain and Fourth President.

CHAPTER XI
GROWING IN FAITH

And God blessed them, and God said unto them, 'Be fruitful, and multiply, and replenish the earth.'
—Genesis 1:28

A growing family required more room. Anticipating additional children, we applied for and were given an apartment in the St. Nicholas Project in the building at 2410 Eighth Avenue. This one was located on the thirteenth floor and had three bedrooms.

In 1956, Deborah was going on two years old and still using the bottle. As we looked down out at the scenery through that thirteenth-story window, she suddenly took the bottle out of her mouth and threw it out of the window. It fell to the ground where we could see it.

I then said to her, "Take a good look at that bottle, because that is where it is going to stay." She looked at me and started to cry. I shook my head. "You may cry if you want, but you threw it out the window, and that's the end of it."

This is how Deborah was weaned off the bottle.

Our Fifth Child

The day after my thirty-ninth birthday was a beautiful, sunny one. My wife had a nice, large ham in the oven for dinner. Our children—Samuel, David, Deborah, and Joseph—were playing in the living room, and Doris was in the kitchen preparing dinner when suddenly she announced, "I have a feeling that this baby is soon to be born."

Doris picked up her small bundle of things in a bag and rushed to the elevator and down to the main floor. I hailed a cab, and off to Harlem Hospital she went. I hurriedly called my father-in-law to come and stay with the children so I could go to the hospital. Mr. Thorpe came in short order, and I went to Harlem, Hospital.

After being there for a while, our fifth and last child was born. At seven pounds, eight ounces, Phillip Charles Joubert, a handsome little fellow with light brown skin, came into this world on the 29th of April, 1961.

I felt very proud to be the father of four boys and a girl. I came to the conclusion that Doris and I were really blessed. After the usual stay, I brought my wife and son Phillip Charles home. He was the crowning glory of our immediate family.

With the arrival of Philip Charles, it became evident that we needed still larger quarters. In 1964, we moved into a six-room apartment: four bedrooms, living room, kitchen, and dining room, all-in-one and one and a half bathrooms on the nineteenth floor of the Drew Hamilton Project on 143rd Street and Seventh Avenue.

We were in for a pleasant surprise. Raymond Jackson, chairman of our Deacon Ministry, worked at a furniture store and convinced our church members to put up the money to buy a lovely dinette set for the parsonage kitchen. He arranged to have it delivered to our new home.

Angels Watching Over Us

Although our family life was joyous and generally peaceful, it was not without its anxious moments. For example, when our son Joseph got old enough to attend school, it was David's responsibility to take him to the bus stop every day. One day as he was attempting to get Joseph on the bus, the door closed and the bus pulled out before Joseph was completely on board. Somehow, the bus ran over one of Joseph's feet.

Imagine my shock when I heard a knock on the door and opened it to find David standing there carrying Joseph on his shoulders because it was too painful for his little brother to walk on that foot.

I immediately got him to the hospital. The doctor examined his foot and had x-rays taken, but thanks be to God, there were no fractures or serious injury. After a few weeks of treatment his foot was as good as new.

When Phillip Charles became of school age, he started attending PS 192 on 133rd Street between Seventh and Eighth Avenues. His older brother, Samuel Jr., was sixteen by this time and was responsible for picking him up and bringing him home after kindergarten class every day. One day, Samuel was late getting there, and this little tiny five-year-old boy decided to walk home *alone* from 133rd Street *ten blocks* up Seventh Avenue to 143rd Street and the

Project in which we lived.

One can imagine how his mother and I felt when we answered a knock on our door and found our tiny son, not much more than a toddler, standing at the door alone.

The Lord does indeed protect fools and little children.

Then there was the great Northeast Blackout of 1965.

I can recall as if it were yesterday. I was a member of the Council of Churches of the City of New York at the time. On this occasion the meeting took place at a church downtown, New York City, on the East side near Fifty-ninth Street. I left home a little after 6 p.m. and took the Eighth Avenue subway to Fifty-ninth Street. I got off and walked over to the church that night. Upon arrival, we assembled in the sanctuary of the church for the formal meeting, which would culminate into a dinner in the Lowes Fellowship Hall.

After the meeting adjourned in the sanctuary, we all assembled in the Fellowship Hall for dinner. Just as we were seated, the light flickered once and went out and came back on for a brief moment and went out again. After a while, those in charge placed candles on all the tables, and we were told that the whole city was without electrical power.

We continued dinner hour as best we could until it was time to go home. When we started to come out of the building between 9:30 and 10, there was darkness all around. The only light came from flashlights wielded by police officers and city buses that were running, since the subway—being electrically powered — was useless.

It wasn't until 3:30 or 4 a.m. that I succeeded in getting on a bus that would take me to Seventh Avenue and 143rd Street in Harlem. By the time I got home it was nearly 5 a.m. The real problem was getting up stairs to my apartment on the nineteenth floor. I was facing the prospect of walking those nineteen flights in pitch darkness, since there was no electricity to power either the elevator or lights for the stairwell. You can imagine my frustration; I had no flashlight, and since I don't smoke, I had no matches or a lighter, either.

God be praised, there was an elderly lady who arrived at the place just about the time I did. She lived a few floors below me — and she had matches. We walked up together. I saw her safely to her apartment, and she gave me the rest of her matches so I could see my way up to my apartment on the nineteenth floor. Isn't God good?

I got home safe and sound just before power was restored in our part of the city, greeted by my wife and children with joy and relief.

As frightening as that was, at least my family had been safe at home. The great Northeast Blackout of 1965 was nothing compared to what we as a family had gone through only a few months earlier.

In late August of 1965, my wife Doris and our five children boarded a jet plane at Kennedy Airport around noon in order to travel to Louisiana to visit my extended family.

The takeoff was without a hitch, and in a matter of minutes we were all settled and enjoying a most peaceful and smooth ride.

The weather was ideal; the sun was beaming down upon us in all its splendor. After awhile, two smiling stewardesses brought our lunch of boneless chicken, rice, green peas, cream cheese and peaches on lettuce, hot roll with butter, milk, coffee and lime gelatin for desert, and ice cold water. The flight was so smooth and peaceful that we had landed at New Orleans several minutes ahead of time and almost before we knew it.

For the next leg of the journey, we boarded a bus to my parents' home in Grand Prairie, where we spent a most enjoyable vacation. The weather was made to order. Days were warm, but not too hot and uncomfortable, and at night there was dew on the grass and a cool breeze that made sleeping most pleasant.

At night my wife and I would stand on the porch and breathe in the fresh air mixed with fresh dewdrops and the fresh and fragrant odor of the beautiful flowers. We also watched the beautiful stars twinkling in their orbits.

The children had wide-open space to run and play and at night they would fall peacefully asleep.

We wish that life be could this way always. Little did we know however that all this happiness was soon to give way to one of the most sudden, unexpected, and dangerous experiences of our lives.

The day before we were scheduled to leave to return to New York, news came over the air reporting that Hurricane Betsy was headed for New Orleans and possibly Louisiana's mainland, which included the Grand Prairie and Opelousas area where we were. There were warnings from the Weather Bureau in

Baton Rouge for people to stock up on fuel and non-perishable food and water and have flashlights and emergency generators ready.

We decided to leave that very day, hoping to get the jump on Betsy. This news came on Thursday. We arrived in Baton Rouge at 9 p.m. and left for New Orleans shortly thereafter, due to arrive at 11 p.m.

Betsy struck about twenty minutes after we left Baton Rouge. We could see the destruction through the bus windows; the wind was high, fierce, and boisterous, uprooting trees, blowing off rooftops and twisting houses — some off their foundation.

The water level was extremely high, and the rain came pouring down like the Great Flood. Water finally entered the engine of our bus, causing the engine to cough and die. Then the lights flickered on and off and finally went out altogether. We were stranded on the highway... caught in the storm.

I fell back on all the scriptures I could utter from memory, especially the Psalms. I prayed as I had never prayed before. There was no other physical help available; I had to reach for the intangible. The three most powerful and destructive elements in the world were united in their fury: wind, water, and in the form of lightning, fire. The only help at a time like this is God; He and He alone can speak to the water and say, "Be calm!" and to the wind, "Be still!" and to the lightning, "behave yourself!" and get favorable results.

Miraculously, the driver of the bus was able to get the motor started again; the lights came back on, and we were moving once more.

The storm grew worse as we moved into what is

known as the eye of the hurricane. It appeared that any moment the bus was going to be swept off the highway. At times, the bus could not move because the wind, rain, and darkness made visibility impossible. The driver would pull the bus over to the side of the road until this visibility improved, allowing us to move on slowly.

Around midnight we pulled in to the bus station in New Orleans and out of the immediate storm. The bus station was dark and crowded—people were lying around on the floor. The water was contaminated, and food was extremely scarce. We had to walk around to keep from falling asleep. There was no place to sit other than the floor and no place to go.

Suddenly it dawned on me, this is Life—Real Life.

Life is not a bed of roses. The sun may shine on your path, but not always. Night is coming. Happiness, joy, and success aren't permanent fixtures in this life. All of us will and must have our day of adversities.

New Orleans was a great city brought to her knees. The rich and the poor were literally on the same level. No amount of money could buy a fresh, cold drink of uncontaminated water. Transportation was virtually at a stand standstill, as the electrical power was off and all the gas stations were controlled by electric pumps.

Large department stores had glass windows were shattered, broken from top to bottom. The streets were littered with broken glass and branches from trees, and telephone poles and electric lines were down and hanging loosely all around. Many homes were badly damaged—some beyond repair.

In the confusion of the evacuation of those living in

lower areas and in the mad rush of thousands trying to reach safety, some families were separated and had no knowledge of the whereabouts of their members until days later.

Around 2 p.m. the next day, we succeeded in getting hotel accommodations, as all planes were grounded and we could not leave New Orleans. When we got thirsty we drank soft drinks that were warm because there was no ice and the water was not fit to drink.

Finally, after two days of living like this, we were winging our way back home.

Since we'd had such a lovely flight along with a nice warm, delicious lunch on the way over we were looking forward to the same on our return flight; we hadn't eaten a decent meal in nearly three days and were anxiously waiting lunch on the plane.

When the stewardess came with our lunch, it was to our utter disappointment made up of cold, tasteless sandwiches, as the facilities in New Orleans for preparing lunch was still out of order. The plane ride was unpleasant as we hit a few air pockets and ran into bad weather.

Finally, the voice was heard over the loudspeaker announcing: "Please fasten your seat belts; we are about to land at Kennedy Airport." Then, the pilot added: "You were entitled to a warm lunch which we were unable to serve you, but arrangements have been made to serve all of you at the airport restaurant."

As we stepped off the plane tired, hungry, dejected, and disappointed, a lovely receptionist met me with a smile and said, "Reverend, how many in your party?"

I replied, "Seven."

She then handed me seven yellow cards and said, "Take these and hand them to the waitress in the restaurant. Each of you will be served a hot lunch."

Needless to say, we enjoyed the best lunch ever. Our spirits were revived. The dark clouds were rolled away. The sun was shining again, and bells of joy were ringing in our souls.

As I now reflect on this contrasting experience, I now have a greater understanding and appreciation for life, the church, and heaven.

I don't mind the storms of life anymore; I know that any day I shall land on heaven's shore. There I will be met by Heaven's Receptionist and given a white stone with a new name written; it shall be my passport that will entitle me to not only a meal, but a permanent mansion in heaven.

Chapter XII
"As For Me and My House..."

Today, I am still blessed with four sons and one daughter, who between them have presented Doris and me with thirteen grandchildren.

Samuel Jr. and his youngest brother, Philip Charles, followed their father into the ministry and are ordained preachers. David Eugene is a regional manager for AT&T, and our third son, Joseph Edward, is one of the finest musicians and pianists to be found anywhere. Deborah is married to a preacher/musician, and is a beautiful singer—just like her mother.

In Closing

As I come to the closing words of this narrative of my life's journey, I am directed to take my stand on the words of the scripture as recorded in 1 Corinthians 15:58, which reads: "Therefore, my beloved brethren, be ye steadfast, unmovable, always abounding in the work of the Lord, forasmuch as ye know that your labour is not in vain in the Lord."

Here, Paul is admonishing the Corinthian Christians to continue steadfast in the work or service of Christ, specifically because of the resurrection of Christ from the dead: "Your labor is not in vain." All the work that we do as followers of Christ will be richly rewarded as stated in 2 Corinthians 5:10: "For we must all appear before the judgment seat of Christ; that every one may receive the things done in his body, according to that he hath done, whether it be good or bad."

Our desire to be with Christ makes us as followers ambitious to please Him (Luke 19:17).

We strive to please the Lord not only because we know He will evaluate our work whether good or bad and reward us accordingly. The person unconcerned about doing good deeds shows a grave lack of vision. That which we sow we shall reap; standing before the Almighty on the Day of Judgment, the believer will be either approved or ashamed. This truth should dramatically change the way we live, for our actions will be evaluated by our Lord Jesus Christ and rewarded accordingly (Matthew 25:31–46).

We are to be steadfast in the faith and practice of the Gospel of Christ in habitual living with unwavering confidence of the coming resurrection known as the Day of Judgment and our eternal reward. "Unmovable" must not be discouraged by opposition or difficulties. We must not allow ourselves to be led to doubt about the complete fulfillment of all that God has declared. "Your labor is not in vain in the Lord" (1 Corinthians 15:58). What we do to obey and honor Christ shall receive a glorious am eternal reward, which is eternal life, ultimately.

This is what I truly believe, and I take my stand.

This is my life's destiny up to this point and time. As I understand the term "destiny," it refers to the divine decree of predetermined connections, of causes and effects in the life of the individual, which results in the achievement of one's ultimate goal based on the choices one makes. Joshua 24:14-15 reads:

> *Now therefore fear the LORD, and serve him in sincerity and in truth: and put away the gods which your fathers served on the other side of the flood, and in Egypt; and serve ye the LORD.*
> *And if it seem evil unto you to serve the LORD, choose you this day whom ye will serve; whether the gods which your fathers served that were on the other side of the flood, or the gods of the Amorites, in whose land ye dwell: but as for me and my house, we will serve the LORD.*

That is my choice: to serve the Almighty God Jehovah. I made my choice to serve God at the age of nine, and that choice determined my destiny. The above scripture was Joshua's appeal to Israel to choose between the true and living God and the many false substitutes.

True religion is a matter of choice with all who heartedly embrace it, and no one ever does or can serve God in spirit and in truth without choosing to do so. As Jehovah is holy, it is impossible to serve Him acceptably without becoming holy—or at least being partakers of God's holiness. Wherever there is a willing mind, one can truly serve God and for Christ's sake be accepted in doing so. It is the duty of all to incline their hearts to serve the Lord.

We should avoid all things that tend to hinder us, and do those things that tend to aid us in this pursuit. We should—and it is right that we should—determine, resolve, and engage to serve the Lord. It is perfectly reasonable that all to whom Jehovah is known should love and obey him.

Rulers and people of faith, as well as other men, women, boys, and girls will soon answer the roll call of death, but their influence will for good or evil live and go down to the end of time and onward to eternity.

It is my purpose that my destiny be in accordance with God's purpose for my life in keeping with Romans 8:28–30, which says:

> *And we know that all things work together for good to them that love God, to them who are the called according to his purpose.*
>
> *For whom he did foreknow, he also did predestinate to be conformed to the image of his Son, that he might be the firstborn among many brethren.*
>
> *Moreover, whom he did predestinate, them he also called: and whom he called, them he also justified: and whom he justified, them he also glorified.*

Loving God distinguishes true Christians from all other men and woman. He that loves God is born of God, and all things work together for good to them that love God.

Those who have been called by God's grace out of the darkness and bondage of sin into the light and liberty of righteousness are made heirs of eternal glory in heaven.

These lines sum up my destiny in Christ: "I am a

"As For Me and My House…"

pilgrim, traveler here with heaven in my view. Heaven is my final destiny; my eternal home."

APPENDICES

Appendix 1:
The Truth about Black History in the Bible

The ancestral home of man—Adam and Eve—was in Africa. In the beginning of Biblical times, Africa included much of what European maps have come to call the Middle East.

In the Bible, there is not one single mentioning of either England or Germany (which did not exist in those days in any event). By contrast, countries of Africa—Egypt, Nubia (present-day Sudan), and Ethiopia—are mentioned again and again. The Old Testament alone cites Ethiopia over forty times and Egypt over one hundred times.

The Garden of Eden account found in Genesis 2:8-14 indicates that the first two rivers of Eden were built in ancient Cush. The Gihon River is cited in Genesis 2:13 as the second river in Eden surrounding the whole land of Ethiopia. Wherever else Eden may have extended, its beginning was within the continent of Africa.

There are many accounts in the Old Testament of blacks and their contributions. A black man, Ebedmelech, took action to save Jeremiah's life (Jeremiah 38:7-13) and was given a divine blessing (Jeremiah 39:15-18). Ethiopians in the Old Testament were wealthy people (Job 28:19). Mary and Joseph took refuge with the child Jesus in Africa. Egypt is in Africa. The idea used to perpetrate slavery and prejudice, that the black race was cursed, is a *lie* and a *falsehood!* In fact, black men and women are fully part of the salvation history within the Bible itself.

For example, Moses himself was an Afro-Asiatic, and he married a black woman (Numbers 12:1-10). The Queen of Sheba was a black African (1 Kings 10:1-10); Sheba corresponds to present-day Ethiopia. Psalm 68:31 says, "Let princes come out of Egypt and let Ethiopia hasten to stretch forth her hands to God." Ethiopia in fact was the second nation in the world to officially embrace Christianity, even before Rome under Constantine!

Those of us in the black church must nonetheless be willing to forgive all mankind who have fallen into the pit of racial hatred and prejudice. This is not a time to get back at, or to get even with. This is a time to show love and kindness and to become reconciled and pray for God's love that all his people will desire His love and be saved from the hatred that destroys the light of God.

In the light of what I have just said, it is time for black men to reclaim their heritage by joining hands and to begin working together in unity and in love to build a viable, caring, and sharing Christian church, home, and community.

Our first step is to surrender our lives to Christ and dedicate and re-dedicate our lives to the work of our church unselfishly.

Then we must pledge to be regular in attendance for Bible training for the work of men's fellowship

The truth About Black History in the Bible

ministry in the community Baptist church.

Appendix 2:
On the Importance of Bible Training and Education

Men who aspire for office in the ministry of the church without sufficient Bible training and orientation are disasters in the making. The Bible says "Study to show thyself approved unto God a workman that needeth not to be ashamed, but rightly dividing the work of truth." (2 Timothy 2:15)

Suppose you had to have your wisdom teeth pulled—would you allow a person who never had any formal training in dentistry to pull your teeth? Or would you rather have someone who had been trained in dentistry and had experience in pulling teeth do the job? Or say that your tonsils had to be taken out. Would you want a throat specialist or just any quack doctor?

None of us would submit our bodies for treatment of any sort to an untrained doctor—someone who likes the title doctor and so puts on a white uniform and hangs a sign out a shingle, but who doesn't even know how to write a prescription. Think about it!

Yet when it comes to the church which deals with our soul and spirit, we take a man with no Bible training and no formal preparation or orientation simply because he is wearing pants, and make him a deacon!

Without sufficient Bible training, that man knows nothing about commitment, tithing, the Holy Spirit, faith, long suffering, patience, prayer, and praying for the sick and shut-in. A deacon must be full of the Holy Spirit and must know how to teach the scriptures. You cannot teach what you don't know.

The challenges confronting the twenty-first-century church calls for men who are spiritually strong and sound in the doctrine of the Christian church. The Muslims are all well trained in the teaching of the Quran, and the Jehovah's Witnesses are well trained in the doctrines espoused by Charles Taze Russell, but in the Baptist church we attempt to operate the church on little more than the Lord's prayer and the Twenty-third Psalm. That's about as much as the average black man knows. That is why we are losing our men to the various cults; they are not prepared to defend the doctrine of the church, and neither are they prepared to lead a soul to Christ.

If the Christian church is to survive in the twenty-first century, we will have to do better than we have been doing. That is why I have you men here tonight to get you ready for Christian living and Christian service to cope with the time in which you now live and the days to come.

The Christian layman must be trained in God's word, the Holy Bible, so he can be strong and in a position to help his son or sons and anyone else's son who is seeking religious knowledge. Man has in him a void that needs to be filled. If it is not filled by the Christian Church, he will get it filled through some other source even if it is the church of Satan himself.

On the Importance of Bible Training and Education

That is the point of the message; we must to do all we can to help prepare our deacons and ministers to cope with the challenges they will surely be confronted with in the days ahead as well as now.

APPENDIX 3:
ON MARRIAGE

First of all, marriage according to the scripture is a divine institution instituted by God almighty Himself.
According to Genesis 2:18–23:

And the Lord God said, it is not good that man should be alone; I will make him a helper comparable to him.

Out of the ground, the Lord God formed every beast of the field and every bird of the air, and brought them to Adam to see what he would call them; and whatever Adam called each living creature, that was its name.

So Adam gave names to all cattle, to the birds of the air and to every beast of the field. But for Adam there was not found a helper comparable to him.

And the Lord God caused a deep sleep to fall on Adam and he slept and He took one of his ribs and closed up the flesh in its place.

Then the rib that the Lord God had taken from the man, He made into a woman and He brought her to the man.

And Adam said: this is now bone of my bones and flesh of my flesh; she shall be called Woman because she was taken out of man.

God performed the first and original marriage,

which was between a man and a woman: a male and a female. It was not between Adam and Adam or Eve and Eve. Consequently, a marriage according to the Holy Bible of divine institution under God can only be between a male and a female, a man and a woman, between those of the opposite sex.

One of the main functions and purpose of marriage is procreation, which can only be through the union of a man and a woman. Matthew 19:4–6 says:

> *And he answered and said to them, Have you not read that He who made them at the beginning made them male and female, and said, for this reason a man shall leave his father and mother and be joined to his wife and the two shall become one flesh. Therefore what God has joined together let not man separate.*

Marriage, which receives God's blessings and sanction, is the marriage of a man and a woman. According to Psalm 128:

> *Blessed is every one who fears the Lord who walks in His ways. When you eat of the labor of your hands, you shall be happy, and it shall be well with you. Your wife shall be like a fruitful vine in the very heart of your house. Your children like olive plants all around your table.*
>
> *Behold, thus shall the man be blessed who fears the Lord. The Lord blesses you out of Zion and may you see the good of Jerusalem all the days of your life.*

On Marriage

Yes, may you see your children's children. Peace be upon Israel. This Psalm focuses on the godly man and wife. Bearing children was a mark of God's blessing, especially upon the wife who is the child bearer to the husband, who is the male and Biblical head of the family.

To this first man Adam, created in the image and likeness of God, He gave dominion over all creation with the exception of the tree of knowledge that grew in the Garden of Eden. In Genesis 1:26, we read: "And God said, let us make man in our image, after our likeness: And let them rule over the fowl of the air and over the cattle, and over all the earth, and over every creeping thing upon the earth."

Inter-marriage of Christians with non-believers is not only forbidden and unlawful, it is unwise. In 2 Corinthians 6:14–16, it says:

> *Do not be unequally yoked together with unbelievers. For what fellowship has righteousness with lawlessness? And what communion has light with darkness? And what accord had Christ with Belial [Satan] or what part has a believer with an unbeliever? And what agreement has the temple of God with idols? For you are the temple of the living God.*

Too may of our Christian women are attempting to build their future on false hope by marrying men who are non-Christian unbelievers, hoping that they will change after marriage. The truth is that in many instances such men grow worse, and more often than not, the woman is pulled away from the narrow path of righteousness. Any couple that attempts to build their marriage without Christ or apart from Christ is building on sand and not on a rock and is headed for a real downfall — and a lot of heartache and trouble.

No couple should get married without having prayed about choosing a mate and without being sufficiently counseled by a spiritually and morally strong, God-fearing, experienced pastor.

APPENDIX 4:
THE SERVICEMAN'S FAMILY

NOTE: *This address was originally delivered at a USO event in 1945 toward the end of the Second World War. While some of the content refers to circumstances and events unique to that time and place, the author believes that it reflects many of the issues still faced by US service personnel today.*

In my work among servicemen from all parts of our country I've heard statements like these many times: "I got a letter from home today, and my family's worried about me—how I feel, how I'm being treated, fed, and so forth." Or, "When I was overseas, my family sure worried about me." Many times I've heard these same soldiers say, "I wish they wouldn't worry about me like that, because when they do, it gets me worrying about them."

Statements like these indicate that the subject of servicemen's family's should be discussed at least from two points of view: from that of the family or home front, and from that of the serviceman. Let us discuss the soldier responsibilities and obligations as they relate to his family at home. In this connection, we must always bear in mind the innumerable handicaps under which our boys are placed when they are changed overnight from civilians to soldiers.

The change even though well and scientifically

planned by our government is nevertheless sudden and drastic. Part of the soldier's training and instruction is that his letters home should contain matters of everyday interest. For example, censorship permitting, he should explain the type of country he is stationed in, customs of the people, historical points of interest. He might mention new buddies he has made, where they are from, or boys he has met from home.

His letters should be optimistic about past war plans. Even though things are not entirely to his liking, the soldier should try to keep his letters from being morbid and unhappy. This is undoubtedly difficult for the soldier at times. I had one soldier tell me that sometimes, try as he would, he couldn't make his letter sound the least bit happy. In these instances he said he just didn't write that day because he thought no letter for a day would be better then one that would cause his family anxiety.

Aside from his letter home, the soldier has other responsibilities. He should pick new friends carefully considering that he is among strangers, and he must guard against forming undesirable habits, such as gambling and drinking to pass free hours away.

Free time should be spent in good, wholesome recreation or worthwhile reading and continuing studies interrupted by induction into the service. Religious affiliations are strongly encouraged by the armed forces, and the serviceman should make a friend of his chaplain, feeling free to take his problems to him at all times.

It has been said repeatedly that there are no atheists in foxholes. The soldier should not wait until

The Serviceman's Family

he is in that foxhole to introduce himself to his Chaplain — and his God.

Every serviceman expects his wife or sweetheart to wait for his return and to be true and virtuous during his separation. Likewise he should remember that the same is expected of him. Marriage vows should be remembered and kept sacred so that the eventual reunion will be joyous and without a feeling of guilt on the part of either the soldier or his wife or sweetheart. In this respect, trust and faith in each other is of utmost importance.

Now as to the responsibilities of the soldier's family, there are many. Don't write to your soldier boy and complain of taxes, long hours of work, rationing, the midnight curfew, and other necessary wartime restrictions. Let him know that you are doing your share of the work, that you are buying war bonds to help win the war now and to help build a future for him. Don't tell him of every headache or cold you have except in the case of serious illness.

Give him details so that he may understand the situation fully. If you feel that a telegram is necessary, don't word it in such a manner as to startle and frighten him. In these cases the family should immediately contact the local Red Cross, who will verify the emergency, and in case of very serious illness when you believe the soldier's presence is necessary, contact the Red Cross at once.

Give him local news of his friends in the church, his lodge or the office, shop or factory. Try to touch on the sports or hobbies in which he was interested when he was home. Tell him who's home on furlough and who has gone into service since he left. If he doesn't get the hometown paper, send him clippings of news that may interest him.

Make your letter happy and entertaining and let him know how much you love him, that you miss him and are waiting for his return.

Above all write him often, every day if possible. I've seen those boys wait for mail call and the look of disappointment on their faces when they don't get that letter from home. Soldiers cherish pictures from home, and an occasional package of cookies, candy (when you can get it or make it), or something you know he likes is a big occasion for him.

The family's financial situation should be discussed with him in a businesslike manner, but don't give him the impression that he must send all of his money home. He needs money for his entertainment and recreation. He has plenty to worry about in the service, and when he left, you accepted the responsibility of managing the family affairs. The wife of the soldier should be careful not to offend her soldier husband by not consulting him on family problems; neither should she keep him worried by making big problems out of routine matters.

On the other hand, don't let him feel that he isn't needed in the managing of the family affairs. Try to use the words "We," "Us," and "Our" more instead of "I," "Me," or "Mine."

When your soldier comes home on furlough, a great responsibility falls on your shoulder. It must be remembered that since he left, he has learned many new things—how to obey orders, march, shoot, and kill. He is almost sure to have changed a little. And he is probably wondering if his family will notice it.

Don't make him feel like a stranger by acting different than you used to and don't just say, "You've changed so much, I hardly know you." Tell him how good he looks and how nice it is to have him home. Don't try to plan his every move on his furlough. Try to determine what he likes to do and do everything in your power to make his furlough full and enjoyable, and when he leaves again, don't make a tragic scene of it.

Let him know that you miss him while he is gone and that you will always be waiting for him, no matter how long he is gone. Send him back to his military duties with the memory of a wonderful furlough and looking forward to his return to his loved ones.

When he finally comes home for good, welcome him with open arms. Let him know how really glad you are that he is back and that the family is again together.

If he should come back from war crippled, or disfigured in any way, the family's responsibilities are indeed great. He must be received in a normal manner and should not be made conscious of his handicap. He must be made to know that this change in his physical appearance makes no difference to his family and that he still occupies the same place he did before he left.

Every consideration without making him feel dependent should be given him in his rehabilitation to his new life. He has given his blood to protect his family and his country and is entitled to every consideration. Let us all assure our soldiers of our faith in them and our love for them. And let us all give careful preparation, prayer, and thanks to Almighty God with our arms and heart wide open when "Johnnie comes marching home again."

Then he will know that his fighting, sacrifices, and bloodshed have not been in vain.

Appendix 5:
Address to the 1960 National Baptist Convention

President Jackson, Honorable Governor, His Honor the Mayor, distinguished guests, and messengers to the Eightieth Annual Session of the National Baptist Convention USA, Inc.:

It is with profound humbleness that I stand here to respond on behalf of the president, officers, and members of our great convention to your heartwarming and most cordial welcome.

We have looked forward to our coming here to the city of brotherly love and sisterly affection with great anxiety and anticipation.

We are indeed happy and overwhelmed with your magnanimous spirit of goodwill.

We have not ceased to marvel over the orderly and hospitable way in which the entertainment committee has gone about its task in helping to facilitate matters to make our stay here joyful and comfortable.

We have come from all sections of America to unite together in Christian Fellowship under the bloodstained, majestic banner of Jesus Christ, as humble, but proud missionary Baptists.

We have come with a prayer on our lips, love in our hearts, and a deep sense of loyalty to our Baptist heritage and the program of this great convention.

We have come with the hope that the theme for this Eightieth Annual Session—and I quote, "that they all may be one," unquote—that this theme will govern our action throughout this session.

We have come to share and to learn, to sing and to pray, to preach and to teach, to challenge and to be challenged. We have come to do the bidding of the master, to do business for the King of Kings and Lord of Lords.

We take this opportunity therefore to say to you, we accept your welcome.

If there ever was time and a people who need and merit words of cheer, encouragement, kindness, hope, and words of welcome, from people of various background, nations, and responsible officials, it is us.

As you know, we are living in an age of unrest, racial tension, bigotry, and discrimination.

In this supersonic jet and space age in which countries are in a mad rush competing with each other in an unprecedented effort to be the first to land a man on the moon and take up eminent domain and conquer outer space for their own selfish purposes, it is gratifying, reassuring, significant, and imperative that we have such an occasion as this.

It is quite obvious to all people of goodwill and sound mind that before we spend too much time and effort trying to control outer space, it would be advisable for us to spend more time and effort learning how to conquer and make use of the resources at our fingertips down here that would help us to live together as brothers in peace, prosperity, and progress.

Secondly, I am delighted to respond to your

Address to the 1960 National Baptist Convention

welcome because this is a great convention. This convention was organized in 1880 and has a membership of 5 million.

Our convention has a program that is forward-looking and geared to the need of its constituents. From 1954 to 1959, our convention has given undergraduate scholarships to nineteen young people. Total cash money given for this purpose is ten thousand and nine hundred dollars.

Our convention also maintains an unrestricted scholarship at Roosevelt University, Chicago, Illinois, which is available for students of any race or nationality who qualify.

Our convention has in recent years established a ministerial retirement fund, whose finances have grown to nearly one hundred thousand dollars.

This convention is not selfish, but is concerned about others in foreign lands. Our foreign mission board is alert and on the job.

In 1959 alone more than seven hundred thousand dollars was raised for foreign missions.

This convention has survived bitter opposition from without and within over the years to this day because it has God for its Father, salvation for its end, the Holy Spirit for its guide, and truth for its rod.

This convention believes in the fatherhood of God and brotherhood of men. This convention believes in the teaching of Jesus Christ, who taught that greatness comes through service.

This convention believes that all men are created equal and are endowed by their creator with such inalienable rights among which are life, liberty, and the pursuit of happiness.

Finally, we are pleased to respond to your neighborly welcome because we have somebody as our chieftain in the person of Dr. Joseph Harrison Jackson. A man with a vision—a man whose heart God hath touched—a man who is brotherly, congenial, and reachable.

He is a scholar, a teacher, a philosopher, a preacher, and a Christian gentleman.

As a statesman and a leader, he has the ability and the personal magic touch of an FDR and L. K. Williams.

As a humanitarian he has the intellect and the clemency of an Abe Lincoln and a Ralph Bunche. As a scholar and a thinker he has the vocabulary of a lexicographer—an Einstein, a Dubois.

As a preacher of the glorious gospel of Christ, he has the persuasive power, eloquence, and the masterful oratory that permeates the heart of the worst sinner, as an Apostle Paul, a Dwight L. Moody.

As a servant of the Most High God, he has the dedication, loyalty, and devotion of a Daniel, a William Tyndale, and Albert Schweitzer.

Now then, we hope our meeting here will serve as a citadel binding us closer together.

We conclude therefore by saying we accept your loyal welcome with sincere gratitude.

APPENDIX 6:
ON MISSIONARY WORK

NOTE: *Throughout his career, Reverend Samuel B. Joubert Sr. has been an active supporter of missionary work abroad. The following addresses were made part of reports delivered to Commission on Foreign Mission at the Empire State Baptist Missionary Conventions in 1979, 1991, 2001, and 2004.*

From the Annual Report, 1979

It is significant that our National Baptist Convention USA, Inc., can trace our concern for foreign mission back to 1880. It was in that year that the foreign mission convention was organized, and it was in 1895 that the Foreign Mission Board of the newly organized National Baptist convention assumed and continued the work so nobly begun. Beginning in Bendoo, Liberia, it had expanded into Nyassaland (now Malawi) in East Africa by 1900.

In 1912 it opened another mission, Suehn in Liberia, until today we serve in Sierra Leone, Ghana, Lesotho, Swaziland, and the Republic of South Africa on the continent of Africa. Our fastest church growth is in Malawi, where we now number 472, bringing our total Africa churches to 677, with membership exceeding 49,000.

Our primary and secondary schools and seminary

serve 1,347 students. Our health service in Liberia and Malawi recorded 20,017 treatments in the past year. Our seminary in Lesotho has 21 students. The Foreign Mission Board is helping to underwrite the salaries of 921 regularly employed workers on the field, with the governments of Sierra Leone, Ghana, Malawi, and Lesotho paying the teacher's salaries on the primary and secondary levels.

Every African country wherein we serve encourages the philosophy of self-help and self-determination. Our role is to preach Christ, alleviate human need, remove the scales of ignorance from their eyes with knowledge and education, and bring healing for their diseases, clothing for their nakedness, and a sense of personal dignity as a child of God.

In the Western Hemisphere, let us be especially mindful of our three churches in Nicaragua pastored and supervised by Rev. Fernando Downs. That unfortunate country is now suffering from the throes of revolt against a family dynasty that has ruled that nation for forty-five years. Let us pray that peace will be achieved and that the people of that land will know the freedom that is the right of every child of God.

The increased contributions in the past year and a half have enabled us to underwrite students from Swaziland, Liberia, Malawi, Sierra Leone, South Africa, Bahamas, and Nicaragua in American colleges and seminaries. It means scholarships for students on a primary and secondary level at our mission schools in Africa and Nicaragua. It means transportation costs for five missionaries to the field. It means the purchasing of new vehicles in Barbados and Swaziland. It means increased salaries for forty pastors in Malawi and the erection of eight churches in the Bantustans in South Africa.

It means added medical supplies, added educational materials, and added publications of missionary study material.

Our help is needed most in the Republic of South Africa. In this benighted land millions of our black brothers and sisters are facing hardships that are beyond the comprehension of the average American. Racially restrictive laws, multiple arrests, housing dislocations, economic exploitations, and tribal relocations have created severe burdens on the average African living in South Africa.

In addition to these burdens there is the new South African Government Policy, which is relocating missions who have lived for three generations in urban areas into areas referred to as Bantustans, which are areas specifically designated for certain tribal groupings. Usually these remote areas are underdeveloped, and the inhabitants thereof are primarily the elderly and the young who are totally unfamiliar with rural living.

The demoralizing effect of relocation on all who are forced to life under these conditions has been recognized by the pastors of the National Baptist churches of South Africa, and they have appealed to us to aid them in erecting churches in their areas as a focal point for worship and spiritual strengthening.

From the Annual Report, 1991

In my opening remarks, I am reminded of the words found in the Fortieth Psalm:

Blessed is the man who makes the Lord his trust, who does not look to the proud, to those who turn aside to false gods. Many who makes the Lord his trust, which does not look to the proud, to those who turn aside to false gods. Many, o Lord, my God, are the wonders you have done. The things you planned for us no one can recount to you; were I to speak and tell them, they would be too many to declare.

Suffice it to say that the God we serve is good. God and His mercy endureth forever.

Now as we approach the twenty-first century, the challenge for missions is greatly accelerated in this changing, compound, complex, social, political, educational, and religious order we are confronted with in our world today.

In St. Matthew 28:18–20 is the Great Commission to the church which says:

Then Jesus came to them and said: all authority in heaven and on earth has been given to me. Therefore, go and make disciples of all nations, baptizing them in the name of the Father, and of the Son, and of the Holy Spirit, and, teaching them to obey everything I have commanded you, and surely I am with you always, to the very end of the age.

Matthew 24:1–14 reads:

On Missionary Work

But he who stands firm to the end will be saved. And this gospel of the Kingdom will be preached in the whole world as a testimony to all nations, and then the end will come.

This authority or official right or power had now been given to Jesus by the Father, and now he was instructing the disciples to go on the basis of that authority. Their field was to include all nations, not just Israel. They were to make disciples by proclaiming the truth concerning Jesus Christ. Their hearers were to be evangelized and enlisted as followers of Christ.

The final words of Jesus as recorded by St. Matthew were a promise that he would be with them always until the very end of the age. Although our Lord did not remain physically, his spiritual presence was with them until their tasks on earth were finished. Likewise, his power and authority along with his presence will be with us until our task on earth is completed.

The question I raise at this point is simply this: Are we really prepared to meet the challenge of missions today in spite of the difficulties involved? Are we willing to give of our time, our talent, and our money? My brothers and sisters, the cry for help in foreign lands is loud and clear—in the person of millions who are dying of hunger, void of proper medical care and educational facilities, political upheaval, and a multitude of other problems, and the time for action is now!

Some time ago a boy fell into an old well. In a short while forty thousand dollars was raised in the small community to bring in the necessary earthmoving equipment for his rescue. In 1937, Amelia Earhart, attempting an around-the-world flight, was reported lost. For the following ten days, our government and others spent over two hundred fifty thousand dollars daily searching for her.

We place higher value on human life under certain conditions. We spend comparatively little on seeking for lost souls in all of its ramifications. We spend ninety-six cents on ourselves out of every dollar and give only four cents to missions.

It is written:

Go ye into all the world and preach the gospel to every creature. (Mark 16:15)

And they that are wise shall shine as the brightness of the firmament; and they that turn many to righteousness as the stars for ever and ever. (Daniel 12:3)

And whosoever shall give to drink unto one of these little ones a cup of cold water only in the name of a disciple; verily I say unto you, he shall in no wise lose his reward. (Matthew 10:42).

Say not ye, There are yet four months, and then cometh harvest? behold, I say unto you, Lift up your eyes, and look on the fields; for they are white already to harvest. (John 4:35)

Fruit is promised for faithful efforts. God has

chosen us and sent us forth in his service, promising fruit as a result of our work.

> *Ye have not chosen me, but I have chosen you, and ordained you that ye should go and bring forth fruit, and that your fruit should remain.* (John 15:16)
>
> *And the master said unto the servant, Go out into the highways and hedges, and compel them to come in, that my house may be filled.* (Luke 14:23)
>
> *And he saith unto them, Follow me, and I will make you fishers of men.* (Matthew 4:19)
>
> *Cast thy bread upon the waters: for thou shalt find it after many days.* (Ecclesiastes 11:1)

Let me attempt to put in a nutshell the mission of the Church.

There used to be an American Missionary worker down in Puerto Rico who discovered this mission soon after arriving on the island. He was young and full of enthusiasm and anxious to do all he could for the poor people he met everywhere, so he wrote his church back home to send him barrels of clothing. He took one particularly good barrel of clothing out to a small church in one rural area that he visited only once a month or so, and proceeded to pass out clothes to all in the place.

He created quite a furor; everybody was talking and laughing at once—and then one of the older men in the little congregation took him aside, put his hand on his shoulder, and said, slowly, "Sir, we are most grateful for all these beautiful clothes, and we thank you for them, but please, couldn't we have the church service first? We've waited so long to hear about Jesus Christ, and it will be so long before you will come again, so please let us hear about Jesus."

That older man was right: the first mission of the church is to bring the good news of Jesus Christ to lost souls, and after that food for the hungry, clothes for the naked, and water and shelter for the thirsty and homeless.

Now the bottom line for the promotion of the Kingdom of God in foreign lands calls for money and yet more money and dedicated missionary workers.

From the Annual Report, 2001

We have come thus far by faith, leaning on the everlasting arms.

Our Foreign Mission Enterprise has its roots centered in the Lamb that was slain from the foundation of the world (Revelation 13:8). It was God's plan before the world began that Jesus Christ the Lamb of God would be slain for humanity's sin, so the names of the believers have been included in the Book of Life from the beginning (Revelation 17:8).

Ours is not a Johnny-come-lately religion. Our faith and practice is founded upon the Lamb that was slain from the foundation of the world. For no other foundation can anyone lay than that which is laid, which is Jesus Christ (I Corinthians 2:11). Jesus Christ is the only sure foundation of human hope, and the true church of Christ is composed of only those who put their trust in Him.

Our Christian witness and Foreign Mission Enterprise is centered in the authority of the Lamb of the Glory, even Jesus Christ, who commissioned the church to go into all the world and preach the gospel to all nations (Matthew 28:187-20). And Jesus came and spoke to them saying:

> *All authority has been given to me in heaven and on earth. Go therefore, and make disciples of all nations, baptizing them in the name of the Father, and of the Son, and of the Holy Spirit: Teaching them to observe all things that I have commanded you: and lo, I am with you always, even to the end of the age.*

Amen.

The Great Commission rests on the authority of Christ because he has authority over all. Therefore, everyone needs to hear his gospel. When Christ gave his first commission to the disciples it was limited to the lost sheep of the house of Israel (Matthew 10:5-6). Now his authority is worldwide and absolute, so this commission was also worldwide. This command is now to the church. So there is never a good reason for the church's failure to reach out and go into all the world.

From the Annual Report, 2004

At the age of nine, I was converted, baptized, and

fellowshipped in the Christian church. From then on, I have been an active worker in the church.

In my home church at that time we had a "missionary circle," as it was called. These women did voluntary work of benevolence in the local church community. The name "Foreign Mission" was exactly that—foreign to the church's program. Some of the churches at that time took up what they called "poor saints offering," which was ten cents per individual. These funds were used to performs acts of benevolence locally—which was limited help.

What can you do effectively with ten cents? The matter of foreign mission was never brought up. Regretfully, that tradition is still in our midst today in some circles, to a certain extent.

Acts 9:16 reads: "During the night Paul had a vision of someone from Macedonia who was standing there and begging him, 'Come over to Macedonia and help us.'" As all of us know Paul's missionary journey's were many. However, the world and everything in it has changed considerably since Paul ventured into Macedonia and other parts.

Paul's missionary strategy was to go into the cities and heavily populated centers and preach the love of God and salvation in Jesus Christ and the cross.

It worked. It produced a missionary crusade that has spread all over the earth. Today, however, we face a changed world. People are more interested in medical and agricultural missions than in evangelical missions.

A few years back the Southern Baptist convention sent out a call for missionaries who could and would specialize in the following missionary work: agriculture, architecture, bookkeeping, bookstore management, business administration, camp direction, chaplaincy, conference directors, dormitory house parenting, English language skills, field evangelism, goodwill centers, mass communications, medicine, dentistry, hospital administration, lab technology, nursing, public health, music education and promotion, church drama, press service, publishing, radio and TV. promotion, school administration, secretarial work, social work, and K-12 education.

In my book soul saving is still at the top of the list, but we cannot ignore the aforementioned worldly matters.

The great work of mission must continue, and after all these years we have made some progress, but most of our churches still treat missions, and especially Foreign Missions, as an unwanted stepchild. We can and must do better. Let us continue to keep Matthew 28:16–20 and Acts 1:8 as our primary focus and goal: winning the lost to Jesus Christ.

APPENDIX 7:
MORE REFLECTIONS ON PAIN AND LOSS: THE STORY OF RUTH

For the record, I say here and now one need not lose his or her zeal nor their faith, because I too have experienced numerous instances of the loss of a loved one, sickness, disappointments, and betrayal by a loved one or dear friend.

There is a way to win the victory over such matters. A good example is found in the book of Ruth. Ruth 1:1–17 reads as follows:

> *Now it came to pass in the days when the judges ruled, that there was a famine in the land. And a certain man of Bethlehemjudah went to sojourn in the country of Moab, he, and his wife, and his two sons.*
>
> *And the name of the man was Elimelech, and the name of his wife Naomi, and the name of his two sons Mahlon and Chilion, Ephrathites of Bethlehemjudah. And they came into the country of Moab, and continued there.*
>
> *And Elimelech Naomi's husband died; and she was left, and her two sons.*
>
> *And they took them wives of the women of Moab; the name of the one was Orpah, and the name of the other Ruth: and they dwelled there about ten years.*
>
> *And Mahlon and Chilion died also both of them;*

and the woman was left of her two sons and her husband.

Then she arose with her daughters in law, that she might return from the country of Moab: for she had heard in the country of Moab how that the LORD had visited his people in giving them bread.

Wherefore she went forth out of the place where she was, and her two daughters in law with her; and they went on the way to return unto the land of Judah.

And Naomi said unto her two daughters in law, Go, return each to her mother's house: the LORD deal kindly with you, as ye have dealt with the dead, and with me.

The LORD grant you that ye may find rest, each of you in the house of her husband. Then she kissed them; and they lifted up their voice, and wept.

And they said unto her, Surely we will return with thee unto thy people.

And Naomi said, Turn again, my daughters: why will ye go with me? are there yet any more sons in my womb, that they may be your husbands?

Turn again, my daughters, go your way; for I am too old to have an husband. If I should say, I have hope, if I should have an husband also to night, and should also bear sons;

Would ye tarry for them till they were grown? would ye stay for them from having husbands? nay, my daughters; for it grieveth me much for your sakes that the hand of the LORD is gone out against me.

And they lifted up their voice, and wept again: and Orpah kissed her mother in law; but Ruth clave

More Reflections on Pain and Loss – The Story of Ruth

unto her.

And she said, Behold, thy sister in law is gone back unto her people, and unto her gods: return thou after thy sister in law.

And Ruth said, Intreat me not to leave thee, or to return from following after thee: for whither thou goest, I will go; and where thou lodgest, I will lodge: thy people shall be my people, and thy God my God:

Where thou diest, will I die, and there will I be buried: the LORD do so to me, and more also, if ought but death part thee and me.

Oh, what faith and what trust and hope in Naomi's God by Ruth! That's the kind of faith in hope, trust, and dedication in the face of adversity that God honors and rewards.

Here was a truly sad and seemingly hopeless situation. Naomi's husband died and left her in a foreign country with two sons. They got married and died at an early age, leaving her with two daughters-in-law. She was jobless, and they were jobless. Naomi decided to do the only wise thing left to do: go back to her country and her God.

One daughter-in-law chose to go back to her parents and her heathen god. Ruth, however, chose to stay with Naomi and go with her to her country and serve her God—the true and living God, Jehovah.

Both Naomi and Ruth left Moab just about penniless. They had hit rock bottom. All they had left was their faith in God, and it paid off.

Orpah did the expected thing and returned home. Yet Ruth unexpectedly stayed with her impoverished mother-in-law. Orpah's action meant that she had left the Israelites and their God.

On the other hand, Ruth's action brought her blessings beyond words. It brought her into the Messiah's family line because she committed her life to God by faith. Ruth was befriended by a relative of Naomi's late husband, a man of great wealth of the family of Elimelech. His name was Boaz. Ruth 4:13 says: "So Boaz took Ruth, and she was his wife: and when he went in unto her, the LORD gave her conception, and she bare a son." Naomi had a grandson as her reward, and Ruth had a wealthy husband and a son as her reward.

But Ruth's reward went beyond that. For you see, Ruth and Elimelech's child—Naomi's grandson, Obed—grew up, married, and had a son named Jesse. And when Jesse grew up, his wife bore him eight sons, the youngest of whom was a great harpist and singer of Psalms—and eventually became King over Israel and Judah.

You know him as King David. And through David's son Solomon was the line of Mary, who gave birth to our Lord Jesus a thousand years later.

When the Lord lays upon you a burden, take it up gladly, for great shall be your reward in Heaven.

APPENDIX 8:
THE BLACK CHURCH

NOTE: *These were included in the original notes for* Life's Cross Roads to Destiny. *The following brief passages are taken from two different sources that have had a profound effect on Reverend Joubert during the course of his life. The first excerpt was written in 1944 by Dr. C. C. Adams, who at the time was the Executive Secretary of the Foreign Mission Board. The second passage, "Words of Wisdom," is excerpted from a 1986 book entitled* Common Thieves *by Dr. Wyatt T. Walker. Dr. Walker is currently National Chairman of Charter Schools and Community Development with the organization Victory Schools. An active worker in the cause of civil rights, he served as chief of staff for the late Reverend Dr. Martin Luther King and was the Senior Pastor of the Canaan Baptist Church in Harlem for thirty-five years. In a poll taken by Ebony magazine in 1993, Dr. Walker was named among the greatest African-American preachers in the country.*

The Ultimate Goal

"It has no less an end that to have God's Kingdom realized on Earth as the only solution to the world's woes.

"The composite and fixed conviction of Christians is that Man's deepest need and ultimate end is God. Without God, men work in the narrow circle of existence. Governments rise only to fall, and human life is a failure with no definite purpose; man's circuit is only completed in God."

Words of Wisdom

"The contemporary American scene in the context of Black America is one of severe crisis. In the last twenty years, we have witnessed visible changes in our everyday circumstances, north, south, east and west. There have been three major civil rights bills.

"The consciousness-raising process precipitated by the presence of Martin [Luther King] and Malcolm [X] has been healthy, if not comfortable in the matter of ethnic differences. We have set aside convenience and hypocrisy that once were forbidden territory.

"Individually, a great deal of 'progress' has been made, but the truth is that many of the gains made during the King era have either been neutralized or nullified by the combination of intransigent racism and the accelerated pace of white progress.

"The bottom line—the reality—is that the black body politic is farther behind its white counterpart than it was prior to the [*Brown v. Board of Education*] Supreme Court Decision of 1954.

"The changes are visible, but they are more cosmetic than they are consequential. Martin Luther King and his movement gave the black clergy and the black church enterprise, a new visibility that it had not had in white America.

"The frenetic activity in the matter of the White vs. Black syndrome in this republic heightened the expectations of the oppressed community beyond our capacity to deliver

"In our painful sojourn in this land, we have had four major institutions that fought for our rights: the black press, black business, black schools, and the black church. The black press is no longer a voice to champion the cause of the downtrodden masses. At the mercy of instantaneous news reporting and electronic news gathering, the black press has been forced into the prostitution of advertising revenues."

APPENDIX 9:
OUR ROOTS

NOTE: *The following sermon was written by Reverend Joubert himself, and was included among the notes for* Life's Cross Roads To Destiny.

Today, we have people of color searching for their roots. They claim that if they can go back far enough in the history of mankind and his culture, they will discover their roots and their authentic identity will be established. In recent years, a black man or woman every so often goes to Africa, looking for his or her identity and comes back claiming they have found the answer, then gather a following in the name of a religion or some other African custom, adopt an African name, attire, and so forth.

Many American blacks are easy prey for this sort of thing, because they have so for so long been subject to such discrimination.

Blacks are the last hired and the first fired; in housing we are pushed aside into the ghetto. In education, predominantly black schools must settle for facilities and curriculum that do not measure up to that of white schools. Throughout America, when it comes to the law, there is one standard for whites and another for blacks. All one has to do is to visit our jails and prisons to discover that all of them are overcrowded with black men and women, boys and girls. Many whites who commit certain crimes are given a slap on the wrist and sent home, while blacks convicted of the same crimes are jailed and sent to prison for years.

Living under such miserable conditions, blacks are eager to listen to anyone who comes as an Angel of Light, saying, "All you need do is read my book, heed my teaching and follow me—and you will find your identity, and *I* will help you overcome!"

Where can I find my identity?

We have to start at the beginning. The Bible says in Genesis 1:1, "In the beginning, God created the Heavens and the Earth."

"In the Beginning… God."

One can start right there. No one was here in the beginning but God—so only what God says about the beginning of the Universe and Man has validity, since he was the only one alive and here in the Beginning. We have to take God's Word for it, and the Bible is God's Word.

The Bible says in Genesis 1:27, "So God created man in His own image, in the image of God he created them; male and female he created them."

Where was man placed? Genesis 2:8 says, "And the Lord God planted a garden eastward in Eden; and there he put the man whom he had formed." Genesis 2:10 reads, "And a river went out of Eden to water the garden; and from thence it was parted, and became into four heads." Genesis 2:13 says, "And the name of the second river is Gihon; the same is it that encompasseth the whole land of *Ethiopia*."

Black people, take note.

Let us look at the facts: God's Word says, "In the

beginning, God created Man and placed him in the Garden of Eden." One of the rivers flowing out of Eden surrounded the Land of *Ethiopia*—which is in *Africa*, "*in the Beginning.*"

Now, the Bible says from the blood of one man—Adam—God made to dwell upon the Earth all nations. Acts 17:26 states, "[He] hath made of one blood, all nations of men for to dwell on all the face of the earth."

Malachi 2:10 asks, "Have we not all one father? Hath not one God created us? Why do we deal treacherously every man against his brother by profaning the covenant of our Father?"

The real, true identity of all of us—regardless of race, creed or color—is found in Adam, the first man who was created by God, who gives to *every* man his identity. So, ultimately, man finds his identity and his "somebodyness" when he finds God. One does not have to go to Africa or anywhere else to find one's identity.

The only One who had the power and authority to give man identity is the *One who created man* – and that *One* is *God*—who is *everywhere.*

Consider the 139th Psalm:

For there is not a word in my tongue, but lo, O Lord, thou knowest it altogether.

Whither shall I go from thy spirit? Or whither shall I flee from thy presence? If I ascend up into Heaven, Thou art there; if I take the wings if the morning and swell in the uttermost parts of the sea, even there shall Thy hand lead me, and Thy right hand shall hold me.

> *If I say, Surely the darkness shall cover me; even in the night shall me light about me. Yea, the darkness hideth not from Thee, but the night shineth as the day; the darkness and the light are both alike unto Thee.*

The Holy Bible in the previous scriptures testifies to the fact that all men are created equal. God is our Father by creation, and Adam is our earthly father because the seed of Adam is in all of us. On that fact, we are *all* brothers and sisters, sons and daughters of Adam and Eve—the first man and woman.

When Adam sinned, he lost his original status with God. Sin brought him down from his holy and happy state, the consequence of which is that all men and women are now sinners. The natural process of childbirth now brings us into the world as creatures of God under condemnation of sin and death.

Thanks be to God, one does not have to remain lost in sin on the way to hell.

The Bible says in John 1:12, "But as many as received Him [Christ], to them He gave the power to become the Sons of God." It is only when one accepts and receives Christ as his or her Personal Savior that you then experience the birth that is not of the flesh, but the spirit—and makes you a son or daughter of God.

John 3:5 says:

> *Jesus answered Verily, verily I say unto thee, except a man be born of water and of the spirit, he cannot enter into the Kingdom of God.*

Our Roots

That which is born of the flesh is flesh: that which is born of the spirit is spirit. Marvel not that I said unto thee, Ye must be born again.

Question: What must I do to receive Christ and be born again into the Family of God?

The answer is clear: read, accept, believe, and obey the words of John 3:16-17:

For God so loved the world that he gave his only Begotten Son, that whosoever believeth in Him should not perish, but have everlasting life. For God sent not His Son into the world to condemn the world, but that the world through Him might be saved.

Revelation 3:20 reads, "Behold, I stand at the door and knock; if any man hear my voice and open the door, I will come in to him and will sup with him, and he with Me."

Salvation is a gift of God to be received; you cannot purchase nor pay for it. Ephesians 2:8–9 says, "For by grace are ye saved through faith, and that not of yourselves. It is the *gift* of God, not of works, lest any man should boast."

Jesus stands at the door of the sinner's heart and says, "Let me in."

Any man—no matter who they are, black, white, brown, yellow, red; rich or poor, high or low—all that is required is that you open the door of your heart and invite him in by praying a prayer such as this:

"Dear Lord Jesus, I know that I am a sinner and I

need a savior, and the Savior I need is You. Here and now, I open my heart to You. I invite You to come in and cleanse me from my sin and take over and be the Lord of my life and abide in and with me forever…"

Then bow your head again, and pray:

"Eternal God, my Heavenly Father, I thank You for the gift of eternal life through Jesus Christ my Lord and Savior, for it is in His Name I pray."

Amen.